A FEW BASIC PRINCIPLES
FOR FINDING MR. RIGHT

- Think of the gym as your personal arena in the competition for a mate.
- When answering a personal ad, meet for coffee, not dinner.
- Don't feel obligated to have sex on the first date. Let's face it: Sex on the first date often equals a one-night stand. However, if he finds himself not having sex on the second or even third dates, you could be asking for trouble.

Gay men are different from straight men. Straight guys may indeed at heart be out to marry a girl just like the one who married dear old Dad, but few if any gay guys are out to marry a guy just like dear old Dad (especially if you believe there's any truth to the domineering mother/weak father theory of homosexuality). And when you boil down THE RULES, they're basically good news for any guy looking for a Stepford Wife.

So what can this book do for you that THE RULES can't? Good question. While no book can turn you into a silver-tongued devil who always says and does the right thing, a book can tell you what *not* to do and when *not* to do it. Let's face it: Finding Mr. Right is a matter of luck. Everything you can do to find him, you should do; it's like playing the lottery. But once you meet him, *that's* when you need a little help saying and doing the right thing to make sure he doesn't evaporate before your eyes. And *that's* what this book is for.

G000145855

Books by Orland Outland

THE PRINCIPLES:
The Gay Man's Guide to Getting (and Keeping) Mr. Right

EVERY MAN FOR HIMSELF

Published by Kensington Publishing Corp.

THE
PRINCIPLES

▼

THE GAY MAN'S GUIDE TO GETTING (AND KEEPING) MR. RIGHT

Orland Outland

Kensington Books
http://kensingtonbooks.com

KENSINGTON BOOKS are published by

Kensington Publishing Corp.
850 Third Avenue
New York, NY 10022

Kensington and the K logo Reg. U.S. Pat. & TM Off.

ISBN 1-57566-626-X

First Revised Printing: May, 2000
10 9 8 7 6 5 4 3 2 1

Printed in the United States of America

For Clint Wyatt

Contents

Introduction:
"The Rules" Don't
Apply

Urban life is about competition for scarce resources—good jobs, great apartments, and fantastic mates. *It's a fact.* You know how to get a good job (learn a skill, develop it, wait for the right opening), how to get a good apartment (read the ads, do every open house, wait for someone to die), but how to get a partner? Sure, you *meet* lots of men, maybe even have sex with lots of men . . . but how many of them stay the night? How many of them do you *want* to stay the night? And of the ones you want to stay the night and who do stay the night, how many of them do you get to see again? And when he's gone, you sit there and think, *Did I do something wrong? Did I say something wrong?*

Some people say it's hopeless, that gay men just weren't made to settle down—even some gay men say it. They've divided their lives into Love from Column A and Sex from Column B, love coming from good friends and sex coming from strangers, and never the twain shall meet. *Bosh.* Sure, it's tough; if it weren't, you wouldn't have bought this book. Sometimes it feels like the competition is too intense, that there are too many people who have more assets than you, that all the good ones are either already taken or aren't available. *Wrong.* There are plenty of desirable men out there who want a relationship as much as you do. What are you waiting for? Oh, yeah. Instructions.

So you picked *that* book up, thinking it would help you in your search for a mate. You knew right off that you'd have to discount some of it, even if the authors told you to do exactly as they did— after all, if you did wear lipstick even while jogging, you would be more likely to get institutionalized than married.

Forget it. "The Rules" don't work for us. See, they're based on one simple fact: Sex, for straight guys, is hard to get. The seventies are over; women don't go home with men an hour after they meet them. Straight guys fully expect a certain amount of wining and dining before they get what they want. But for the average gay man in the average mid- to large-sized city, sex is about as hard to get as a bag of Pepperidge Farm cookies. *Withholding the goods* is the cornerstone of "The Rules," and it's in Rules Girls' best interest to get as many other women playing the game the same way they are. It's the new millennium, kids. People are having sex again, and if you try to convince a gay man that abstinence is the road to happiness, you'll find yourself on a very lonely road indeed. The point is not to withhold nookie; this will only leave you single and horny; the point is to *use nookie to your advantage.* More on this later.

More bad news: Those girls actually recommend that you study the movie *Love Story* "like the Bible." Knock knock: Hello? *She dies at the end!* What kind of happily-ever-after is that? Of course, considering that part of "The Rules" is about withholding as much information about yourself as possible, maybe the ultimate Rules Girl success story is to die of a glamorous illness before he discovers all those secrets you've been keeping, so his vision of you as Supergirl never dims. The plan here is to use your encyclopedic knowledge of old movies (you *are* a gay man, after all) to good advantage herein; however, rest assured that *Love Story* is not on the syllabus.

Here's more news you don't need: *Gay men are different from straight men.* Straight guys may indeed at heart be out to marry a girl just like the one who married dear old Dad, but few if any gay guys are out to marry a guy just like dear old Dad (especially if you believe there's any truth to the domineering mother/weak father theory of homosexuality). And when you boil down "The

Rules," they're basically good news for any guy looking for a Stepford Wife.

Which is not to say that some of "The Rules" don't apply: Though this may come as a surprise to some people, gay men are still men. They're just as quickly scared off by the "M" word as a straight guy, just as turned off by a raw display of need. Later on we'll review some of "The Rules" that apply universally.

So what can this book do for you that "The Rules" can't? Good question. While no book can turn you into a silver-tongued devil who always says and does the right thing, a book can tell you what *not* to do and when *not* to do it. Let's face it: Finding Mr. Right is a matter of luck. Everything you can do to find him, you should do; it's like playing the lottery. But once you meet him, *that's* when you need a little help saying and doing the right thing to make sure he doesn't evaporate before your eyes. And *that's* what this book is for.

Are you ready to join the competition? Are you ready to get the man you desire and deserve? Great. Let's go on, through the phases of the competition: Finding Him, Getting Him, and Keeping Him.

▼1

FINDING HIM

1

The Graduate Principle

So you've spent years going out on Friday nights, alone or with friends; you've picked up more tricks than David Copperfield, and you're ready to settle down with someone.

Or are you?

Being ready for a relationship involves more than deciding you want one. You may be fooling yourself, frankly, thinking that a relationship is what you want when what you're really looking for is . . . Well, take the quiz below and see what it is you really want.

1. I want a man in my life to
   a. give me something to do every Friday and Saturday night.
   b. be romantic with.
   c. complete me.
   d. share my interests and ambitions.

2. Love means
   a. never having to say you're sorry.
   b. the solution to all my problems.
   c. I don't have to develop a social life, because I'll be with HIM.
   d. a lot of hard work and compromise.

3. The man I marry will be
   a. everything I ever wanted in a man.
   b. rich beyond my wildest dreams.
   c. fanatically devoted only to me.
   d. someone not entirely unlike myself.

It really is important to know what you're looking for here. If you think finding a man will solve all your problems, you are asking for trouble. A man cannot fix your life. A man cannot give you a life. A man cannot complete you. You've got to be a whole person yourself before you can really connect with another man. You may say you want "romance," but what is that, exactly? Just because two people think holding hands on the street is wonderful, does that really give them anything in common? Does it give them a reason to want to hold each other's hands other than that they want to be held? "Romance" isn't the goal—meeting someone you can feel something for is the goal; *then* the romantic feelings will come.

Another question to ask yourself: How do I feel about forsaking all others? If you live in a big city, sexual opportunity is yours on every corner. If you find that you simply cannot turn down every attractive invitation you get, maybe you need to spend a little more time playing the field before you start looking for a significant other.

This is *The Graduate* **Principle:** The last thing anybody wants is to make it to the altar only to have your spouse-to-be whisked away by Dustin Hoffman pounding on the glass. Think about it: Don't go into a relationship that's only going to end in tears because you find out deep into it that it's not what you want after all.

▼2

The Danielle Steel Principle

Before you go you need to sit down and make a list. Title it "What Do I Want?" If your sole answer is "a relationship"— *bzzzz! Wrong!* The English translation of that is "any warm body." If you really meant that, you'd already be shacked up with the guy who mops up the back of the dirty book store. Of course, at the opposite end of the spectrum are those guys who will be single until they die because they'll still be waiting for JFK Jr. to realize he belongs on the other side of the fence.

Of course you want a relationship, but whom do you want it with? The first step is to write down a description of your dream man, but the second step is to *be realistic.* Yes, our culture continuously feeds us pictures of grade AAA beefcake to get us to buy everything from underwear to microwaves, so it's easy to become convinced that you'll never be happy unless you end up with a guy from the International Male catalogue who also happens to be a brilliant, witty med student putting himself through school by modeling.

This is the **Danielle Steel Principle:** Don't let the perfect man of your dreams become the only man you'll ever marry. Settling for less than you want isn't the point, but accepting that dream men are usually just that is a good start toward getting a real man. Years of experience has taught some of us that not only does the very best sex not come from the very best bodies, but that often the difference in bed between a marble statue and a buff dude is that the dude is warmer (sometimes).

At this point we need to talk about something gay men don't like to acknowledge: The Food Chain. You know what it is—there's always someone a little younger, a little more muscular, a little better hung, a little more tan than you. And every man has the urge—some to a small degree, others to a greater degree—to trade up on the Food Chain at every opportunity. It's in the male gene, part of what makes so many men avoid commitment—the knowledge that something a little better is always just around the corner. (This goes back to **The Graduate Principle**—if you can't break free of that desire to keep trading up the Food Chain, maybe you aren't ready for romance.)

Part of being realistic is figuring out your place on the Food Chain. Now, on this Food Chain, every fish wants to be swallowed by a bigger fish. Everybody wants to end up with someone a little better than they have any right to expect. The key to actually ending up with a mate is to know what you can reasonably expect to get. If you are a severely overweight video store clerk, you *could* refuse to date anybody but handsome, chiseled doctors, but it will probably be just you and Dr. Quinn on Saturday nights for the rest of your life.

Gay men long ago discovered that the secret of happiness was to become the object of your own desire. Love men with giant muscles? Well, most guys with giant muscles want *other guys* with giant muscles, so why not start spending more time at the gym growing some yourself? This is what differentiates the sexual Food Chain from the natural one: *You can change your place in it.*

Take a look at gay couples you see on the street—often they look alike; it's not because they've morphed into a single, nauseatingly happy unit, but because they were *already* alike when they met. Opposites attract, but composites connect. Those two guys look alike because they share the same rung of the Food Chain. If you find that you can't be happy with the men you can get at your rung of the Food Chain, then you need to take steps to make yourself a desirable mate for someone higher up the chain. Otherwise you're dooming yourself to eternal spinsterhood and, worse, you'll find yourself becoming that most frightening of prospects: a Bitter Old Queen.

Make a list of everything you want in a man. You know how you are: You read the personal ads, and there he is: an avid movie buff, a good cook, fond of snuggling during long candlelit walks on the beach etc., etc., BUT he's 5'5" (or 6'6"), bald (or hairy), top (or bottom)—in short, NOT what you're looking for. By process of elimination, you come up with a list of what you *are* looking for. Go ahead. Build your dream man, and caption him "Just What I Ordered." Be prepared to accept someone who's got about 75 percent of what you're looking for.

Does this sound cold? Calculating? Am I really literally telling you to make a list and check off little boxes? *You bet I am.* You want this guy to be someone who's going to interest and excite you for years to come, so there's no point in going out with someone who doesn't do either for you just because you're lonely and he's a "nice guy." Is there any more damningly backhanded compliment than "he's really nice?" Doesn't that really mean "There's nothing horribly wrong with this guy and I'm desperate so even though there's nothing about him that trips my trigger I'll date him anyway?" *You are wasting your time!* You will find yourself drifting into a relationship with Mr. Nice and then find yourself wondering why you're dissatisfied.

Don't expect to get it all, but you know you won't be happy unless he's got the qualities that make you sit up and take notice. *Be honest with yourself.* You may say out loud that "size doesn't matter" because you don't want anyone to think you're a size queen—but if you are, you're going to have to acknowledge it. Say it loud and say it proud: "I WANT A BIG ONE!"

Now you know what you want. Excellent! It's time to start looking for it.

▼3

The *Auntie Mame* Principle

I have terrible news for you. Your knight in shining armor is not about to break into your apartment anytime soon. *You are going to have to leave the house.* Mail order is not an option. You know your usual avenue: the bar. Let's face it: In the gay community, the places we look for sex are also the places we look for love. Don't think that the usual avenues are hopeless: One of the happiest couples I ever knew met in a sex club. Let's come back to those later, though. There are certainly other avenues.

If you are looking for more than sex, you are looking for someone who shares some of your interests. That's right: time to make another list. When we get to the personal ads later in this book, we'll discuss how to write an ad, but the list you're making right now (aren't you?) will prove handy later. Remember: "Long walks" and "candlelit dinners" are not interests. If you and Mr. Right end up sharing LWs and CDs, it will not be solely because you both think they sound wonderfully romantic, but because you have enough in common to develop real affection for each other.

It's just as important to remember that while shared interests are crucial, if you do happen to meet somebody, and you find he has a fanatical interest in, say, boxing, don't pretend that you do, too, when you don't.

This is the *Auntie Mame* **Principle:** You are a gay man. You have seen *Auntie Mame.* You remember what happened to Roz

Russell when she pretended she was an accomplished horse-woman. Behave accordingly. Nobody ever approached someone and said, "You just made a complete fool of yourself; would you like to go out sometime?"

▼4

The Frog Prince-iple

Now you are ready to begin looking. You have decided you are ready, and that, therefore, love is just around the corner. You put your first personal ad in, or take your first class, or any of the other options presented below. And you sit back, and wait for love to come.

Ahem. I did tell you that mail order was not an option, didn't I? In the age of immediate gratification, it's hard for us to conceive of something we can't have just by deciding we want it. Bored? Charge a new wardrobe! Horny? Down to the sex club for some junk food intercourse. Hungry? Pick up the phone and a pizza will manifest itself.

Love, alas, does not work this way. Knowing what you want is not the same as being able to get it. I'm warning you: This is a process that is going to take a lot of time. This is the **Frog Prince-iple:** You are going to have to kiss a lot of frogs (and be a lot of other men's frog yourself) before one of them turns into Prince Charming.

You need to think of love as a lottery. Everything you do to find it is like buying a lottery ticket. Chances are no one ticket will pay off, but if you buy enough tickets, your odds increase exponentially. Each frog you kiss is one more lottery ticket you've bought that didn't pay off. When you lose in the lottery, do you spend the rest of the week kicking yourself, wondering what went wrong?

Of course not. Now, in love, you do make mistakes and you can learn from them, but when you meet someone and something goes wrong, don't kick yourself! Learn from your mistake, and move on. How many other people bought tickets in that lottery and didn't win? You're not the only one to strike out today.

Don't give up. This is going to take some time. If you've made your list, and you've built your dream man, you know that when you find him (or 75 percent of him), it's going to be worth the wait.

The Mr. Chips Principle

"Take a class!" It's the siren song of all single people fed up with bars. Why the hell do you think The Learning Annex is still in business? The amazing secrets of salesmanship it imparts? The wisdom of Uri Geller, available nowhere else?

Taking a class is a great way to meet people. There're no threateningly sexual overtones, you get to meet new people, and you learn something in the process—that is, unless you're spending all your time staring at the instructor. In fact, the **Mr. Chips Principle** states that a good-looking teacher can be a boon to you: It gives you an icebreaker with your fellow gay student(s) during break time. And who knows? Seeing as how you're not a tender undergraduate and he's not worried about tenure, since most extension class teachers are hauled in from real life rather than academe, you may even get lucky with teacher. (Don't count on it, though.)

The *Auntie Mame* **Principle** comes into play here: Don't take a sailing class because you want to meet J. Pierpont Finch III, or because you think guys with sailboats are sexy. You need to have *some* interest in the subject being taught, or you're setting yourself up for, at worst, grief, at best, boredom.

Of course, the kind of class you take will certainly determine the kind of people you meet. If you'd rather die than date Bill Gates, don't expect to find love in your Advanced Windows 95 class. Don't be surprised to find a roomful of old hippies in a basket-weaving class, or a lot of Stevie Nicks clones in a poetry-writing class.

Also, don't be discouraged if you start the class and everybody in it is yucky-looking. Remember: These are all people who can introduce you to their friends, some of whom may be most un-yucky.

The important thing is to have fun, learn something, and meet new people. You may meet someone on campus who isn't even in your class! Taking a class is one of the best lottery tickets, because even if you strike out on the romance side, at least you've gotten a little personal growth out of it.

The Bookworm Principle

If you're reading this book, congratulations: You're in the minority of people in this country who still read books. Why not put this accomplishment to work by cruising your local bookstore? The **Bookworm Principle** states that if you read, and he reads, well, there's a rare interest you have in common right there. Don't judge him just because he's got the latest John Grisham in hand; everybody needs a good airplane read now and then (though if it's the latest Danielle Steel, you might want to think again). For all you know, he's been pulling all-nighters writing his dissertation on Yeats and is ready to blow off a little steam, literarily speaking (as well as the other way, too). At a certain point, you'll get the signal—you'll catch his eye, or you won't. He'll be gay, or not, interested, or not. Make things easy for him. Find your way to the fiction section and pick up a book like Robert Rodi's comic novel *Fag Hag*—it shows you've got a sense of humor, and it has the word FAG in fluorescent orange letters visible several miles away. Subtlety can come later.

Readings are a wonderful way of meeting people. The hardest thing about meeting someone you're attracted to is finding an opening gambit, especially if he's cute enough to make you nervous. At a reading, you know that everyone else in the room is as interested in the author doing the reading as you are, which gives you the greatest advantage you can have when meeting someone:

something to talk about right from the start. Have you read his other books? Aren't they great? Which one is your favorite? Nothing brings two people together faster than being excited about the same things.

The Eliza Doolittle Principle

If you are a gay man, chances are you belong to a gym. If you live in an urban area, you probably belong to a gay gym. You know how competitive it is out there, and you know that without those bulging muscles, you'll never be at the top of the Food Chain. For many of us, the gym is a dispiriting place, where there's always someone with bigger muscles, a deeper tan, wearing the exact same size and brand of jeans we wear yet looking entirely different in them than we do.

Be of good cheer. It's time to start thinking of the gym as your personal arena in the competition for a mate. It has the advantage of a bar (it's full of horny, sweaty gay men) without the disadvantages (nobody is smoking and the only thing being served at the bar is a smoothie, so nobody is going to throw up on your shoes), the advantages of a sex club (you can see your potential date fully undressed) without the disadvantages (if you connect with someone at the gym, someone higher up the Food Chain than you is not going to sweep by and steal him away). You see? *What more can you ask for?* But, you say, I'm a 98-pound, or a 300-pound, weakling. No matter. Remember: *The Food Chain is not static; you can change your place on it.*

This is the **Eliza Doolittle Principle:** Six months of concerted effort at the gym will give you *some* results—and don't think nobody is noticing. Gay men are constantly judging themselves, constantly comparing themselves to other gay men. If they see you three times a week for six months, and one day they realize you now have biceps, they may not jump up and shout, "I think she's got it!" but believe me, they're *all* noticing. Do not be surprised if you suddenly find yourself dating men who previously wouldn't give you the time of day (and when that happens, try not to gloat).

(Fashion note: If you are just joining a gym, chances are you are not in shape. Therefore, do not begin your gym career by purchasing a body-hugging unitard from the International Male catalogue unless you, *and all your friends,* are absolutely sure you will look like an International Male model when you put it on. Once you've got the Body of Death, you can do what Eddie Murphy did in *The Nutty Professor:* Go into the store and shout "Spandex! Everything spandex!")

Cruising at the gym: The rule at the gym is the same as it is anywhere: Try not to stare. It makes you look (a) needy, and (b) like you've never seen a body like that before in your life. Sure you have—just not in person. After you've been going to the gym for a while, you'll adjust to the higher beef percentage. The same is true in the locker room: You learned in high school to be discreet when checking out other guys' packages. There is no reason for you to stop now. Staring openmouthed at a gigantic penis is not going to get you an invitation to do anything with it.

It's always acceptable to try to make eye contact with anyone you find desirable; however, try to do so when both you and he are between sets. When you are in the middle of your set, you should be concentrating on feeling your muscles work and on maintaining good form, *not* on the incredible ass in neon spandex crossing your field of vision, nor should you be trying to catch the eye of someone currently attempting to power-lift 200 pounds.

Don't be shy about your rights: He may be ten years younger, two inches taller, and have 15 percent less body fat than you, but you both paid exactly the same amount of money to belong to this place. You will find jerks at the gym just as you find them every-where. See the guy who gets on the chest press, pushes once with a great exhalation, then looks around scowling as he strokes his pecs with his hand? Walk right up and ask if you can "work in;" this is a gym phrase that means you want to get a set in on a machine while someone else is resting between their sets on the same machine. He will probably not have the nerve to say no, though his whole shtick is all about repelling such requests. You will make an enemy of him, but he's a jerk anyway, and this will help you build confidence when it comes time to start approaching handsome guys who aren't jerks.

Opening lines are not easy to come by. "Come here often?" sounds absurd; of course he does! Informal surveys have proven that should you find yourself smiling at someone and he smiles back, the best way to go from there is to ask, "Can you spot me?" This is another gym term; it means asking someone to stand at your head while you do a chest press so that he can catch the barbell should you fail before getting it back where it belongs. Of course, you might want to be able to press more than, say, 20 pounds before you ask someone to do this.

However: This leads us to one of those excruciatingly important stop-everything caveats: DO NOT under any circumstances try to show off by lifting more weight than you know you can lift properly for the proper number of sets. *You will both hurt and embarrass yourself when you fail.* It is *not important* how much weight the steroid-bloated monster next to you is pumping. The point is to lift as much as you can until you're strong enough to lift a little more. End of lecture.

Ending it: A relationship with someone you meet at the gym is not unlike dating someone you know from work: If it ends, you still have to see each other on a regular basis. Many relationships that start at gyms end amicably not because both parties adore each other but because both parties have paid huge amounts of money for their membership and are both unwilling to pay again somewhere else, or give up the potential new dates still to be found where they met you. If you're the obsessive type, and you know you're going to become suicidal when you see the man who dumped you making out in the steam room with someone else, you might want to consider joining a straight gym in the first place and concentrating while there on your body and not your social life.

The *Working Girl* Principle

We all know people who greet us with a wild expression, who gasp breathlessly, "I haven't a minute to myself!" as if this were some kind of accomplishment. They work like dogs not because they have to, but because they like to. For some of them, it's about really enjoying what they do. But for many, let's face it: It's about avoiding having to deal with their personal lives, or lack thereof. After all, if you don't give yourself time to date, well then, you can't worry about not meeting Mr. Right, can you?

These people need therapy, and I am not a licensed therapist. We will leave them to their own devices and concentrate on *you,* the unwilling workaholic. You'd like to get out and meet men, but you really truly don't have time for it. And you know that an office romance is a no-no—don't you?

However, work can still provide romantic opportunities; thus, the *Working Girl* **Principle:** Melanie Griffith found love with Harrison Ford in *Working Girl,* a perfect cinematic example of what I'm talking about: They worked together, but not for the same company. Socializing at business functions, working late hours together on a big deal, they found themselves in love. Of course, the likes of Harrison Ford are not to be plucked from the vine so easily as that, but we're using movies as a guide here, not a prophecy.

Most careers offer you the opportunity to meet other people in the same profession. *Take advantage of every one of these.* Seminars, workshops, meetings of professional organizations are all events you can convince your boss (the one who is, after all, responsible for your lack of a personal life) are necessary to your professional development. She doesn't need to know you're also trolling for dates.

Of course, unlike our careers, our emotions are sometimes beyond our control. Falling for someone you work with (or, worse, someone you work for or who works for you) is love at its most inconvenient. Don't think for a minute that your brilliant strategems ("Brad is on vacation in Aspen this week and Bill is at a seminar in Tahoe!") are fooling anybody. *How convenient* that the two gay men in the office are both out of town the same week.

Think of it this way: How long did it take you to find out how much money everybody else in the office is making? Take that amount of time, divide it by four, and you'll know how long your torrid forbidden romance is going to remain a secret.

If it even *begins* to look like more than a fling between two people with no lives outside the office, one of you is going to have to get another job. It's not a question of your being gay; it's a question of survival: If you're keeping a dark personal secret, and someone finds out without your telling them, they're going to lose respect for you. The other people in your office are going to look at you, and while they may not smirk on the outside, they are on the inside. You—and your work—will never be taken seriously again. You and Brad are either going to have to bring the relationship out in the open and face the music, or get the hell out of there.

▼9

The Now, Voyager Principle

Even if you do have no life outside work, you are entitled to two weeks of vacation every year. I suggest you take them. Take one week for pottering around old New Hampshire churches, if that's your thing, but if, unlike the closeted movie stars who just say it to hide what's really going on, you *really* don't have time for a personal life, you might think of taking the other week for raw, unadulterated fun.

Bette Davis took a cruise on the advice of her psychiatrist and she got Paul Henried out of it. But that was just a movie. The *Now, Voyager* **Principle** is simple: Do not expect a shipboard romance to turn into a lifetime commitment. However, one week of passion in Provincetown and fifty-one weeks of loneliness beats the hell out of fifty-two weeks of loneliness, hands down.

It is almost impossible not to get lucky in a gay resort community. Everyone is there for the same reason you are: a zipless good time. Of course you're looking for Mr. Right, but you haven't found him yet, have you? So why not take a trial run with someone you'll probably never see again. It'll be fun, and it'll be good practice for the real thing.

In every gay resort town, you will find friendly natives, most of whom have moved there so they can have sex with *you*. You may be too grand to date a busboy back home, but when the busboy has biceps like *that,* who are you to turn your nose up at him?

Relax. It's a vacation. The whole point is to do what you don't do at home.

Of course there is the extremely remote possibility that you will meet someone who lives on the opposite coast, the two of you will fall madly in love, you will visit each other frequently in the months after your fling, and eventually one of you will relocate. DREAM ON! Unless this guy really is 100 percent of everything on your list, you're making your life a lot more difficult than it has to be. You're grasping at straws because it's been so hard to find someone at home. A fling is a fling is a fling. Accept it for what it is, enjoy it, and accept it when it ends.

Going with a friend can be a boon or a curse. Face it: You will need separate rooms. If you have never taken this kind of vacation before, you may *think* you can get away with one room ("We'll save so much money!"), but you'll be sorry. You will find that everyone you meet wants to go to your place (unless you have your own place, in which case the curse won't take effect), and you will find your roommate always has plans that don't include staying out of the room all night. It's great to have a companion to fill the surprising number of hours that can't be filled looking for sex; nonetheless, make sure you've both got room to maneuver at night.

▼10

The Mr. Goodbar Principle

Some enchanted evening, you may meet a stranger. However, chances are, you'll go home with him, have sex, and never see him again. This is the **Mr. Goodbar Principle:** Don't expect to find love where you go looking for sex. As Diane Keaton found out in *Looking for Mr. Goodbar,* this only leads to grief.

You are a man. You need to get laid. You cannot afford to wait for Mr. Right to come along before you have an orgasm with another man. I'm not saying you *can't* find love with someone with whom you are only partly acquainted through a hole in a wall for the first fifteen minutes of your relationship, just that you probably *won't.*

There is just something about sexually charged environments that isn't conducive to starting a relationship. Bars aren't conducive because you're half tight by the time you start talking to someone, and few people are as scintillating in their alcohol-soaked stupor as they think they are. Sex clubs aren't conducive because there's so much eye candy that it's hard to concentrate on one person in a nonsexual way for very long. When you do go out to get laid, think of it the same way you think of going to a gay resort: You're going out to have fun, not get married.

Now, on the surface, this may not have much to do with catching a mate, but this is a good time for a little sexual etiquette lesson. Too many gay men are going to these establishments and acting like pigs. However remote your chance of meeting Mr. Right through a hole in the wall, there is nonetheless *always* a chance for love. When he first sees you, you want him to see you on your best behavior, no? Then read on.

Because of Health Department regulations, most of these establishments offer little in the way of privacy. This means that you and your business—or anybody else and their business—are up for public inspection at all time. Now, some people are into group sex. They welcome dozens of hands cutting into their duet, regardless of what those hands are attached to. Fine! Be a glutton for attention, if that's what you want. However, if you're on the other end of the hands, try to show a little restraint when you see that your intrusion is not necessarily welcome. He may not push you away, but that may be because he's distracted by the sex he's finally having with the man he chased around for the last half hour, not because your attentions are welcome. Stand a little ways away and wait for eye contact before making your move.

Accept rejection gracefully. This is a lesson we'll spend more time on later in the process; rejection is something you will find to your dismay that you will get as well as give during your search for Mr. Right. If he doesn't want you, *he doesn't want you!* "No means no" isn't something you usually hear from men; nonetheless, the principle still applies. Don't embarrass yourself looking for a chance to sneak into line and join his party.

If you see two people making an attempt to go one-on-one in what is probably the most private space they can find, you do have the right to stand there and stare unabashedly as they go about their business; however, if you want to be polite, you won't do this. Moreover, you *especially* won't decide that one of them is hot enough for you to snatch away from his current partner. "Cutting in" is a time-honored way of whisking someone away from their current date; nonetheless, it's still not very nice. Sex clubs are open late: If he's still horny after he's done with his current partner, and he finds you desirable, don't worry: You'll end up with him sooner or later. End of lecture.

The *Pretty Woman* Principle

Some of you may be shocked—*shocked!*—by this chapter. But the fact of the matter is, we all get lonely. The search for love gets to be tiring, and there are times when we can't even find sex, let alone love. This is why the back pages of many local gay periodicals contain ads for what are euphemistically called "escorts."

There is nothing wrong with calling an escort. You're lonely, you're horny, you've got one hundred or so extra dollars. An escort who's good at his work will not only please you sexually, but will also be friendly and even affectionate. You may find that while you thought you were calling to order in sex, you were really calling to have a little physical affection delivered.

The important thing to remember here is the *Pretty Woman* **Principle:** Just because Julia Roberts fell in love with Richard Gere, don't think that the friendly escort you hire is going to fall in love with you. Men who are successful as escorts are successful because they are able to keep an emotional distance from their work—this means you. Also, while he may be Julia Roberts, you are probably not Richard Gere. Remember: Richard didn't *have* to pay for it!

Don't kid yourself into thinking that you can turn this into a romance by calling him over frequently. *Paid sex is not a relationship!* By allowing this half-relationship to become a substitute for the boyfriend you've come to believe you'll never find, you're guaranteeing you'll never have a normal romance. Enjoy what you can get from escorts, but never kid yourself into thinking that you can pay for love.

You may find yourself becoming friends with your escort. This happens when you go into the transaction with a light heart, accepting what you can get from it, and not expecting more. He's a gay guy, too, you know, who moved to the city with many of the same expectations you did. And remember: If he's cute enough to be doing this for money, he's probably got a lot of cute friends he can introduce you to!

▼12

The Crystal Allen Principle

On the opposite end of the spectrum, don't let anybody else think they can buy your love, either. It may be pleasant to think of Mr. Right as coming with all the qualities you want in a man, plus a big fat wad of cash, and we all laugh about marrying for money. And if you're young, and impressionable, and someone with a lot of money comes along and offers to shower you with it, well, the temptation can be great.

This is the **Crystal Allen Principle:** You remember Crystal, aka Joan Crawford, in *The Women*. That scheming shopgirl stole Steven Haines away from (admittedly drippy) Mary Haines, not because she loved him but because he had a lot of money to spend. Well, as you remember, by the end of the movie Crystal has neither job nor man, and the same could happen to you. Allowing yourself to become dependent on someone else financially is asking for trouble! Face it: If he's out shopping for what his money can buy, he may very well find something a little higher up the Food Chain than you, and you'll be out on your ass before you can say, "Boo."

Such unequal relationships never last. You're far better off making your own money, or learning to live without so much money, than hoping he'll never tire of you.

▼13

The Woman-Never-Gives ... Principle

Some of your friends will sniff haughtily when you tell them you're thinking about putting a personal ad in the paper. "It's the last refuge of the desperate," they'll say. "Lonely old men and incarcerated criminals. Do you know anybody who's met through the personals?" they'll ask damningly. "Nooo . . . " you'll answer, embarrassed.

But you do. The thing is, when you ask a couple how they met, the last thing either of them wants to admit is that they met through an ad. So they'll say, "Oh, we met on a deserted beach in the tropics" or some such bosh, but the fact is, people do meet through ads—especially gay people, for whom until recently many social avenues for meeting people weren't available. You can succeed in the personals if you do it right.

Personal ads are like the *Enquirer* and the *Star:* Everybody looks down on them, but everybody reads them. And if you're out to meet someone with similar interests (and you should be), what better way than to announce those interests to the world? The key to success is writing the best possible ad. Here are some pointers.

Tradition has it that an ad allows you to be dishonest. That they do; when nobody can see you, they can't tell if you're lying. The problem is, the whole point of the exercise is to meet someone for the first time, and if you've written that you're 6'1", 180 pounds, twenty-five years old, and hung big, and you're *really* 5'7", 300 pounds, fifty years old, and have difficulty finding it when you have to pee, you're setting yourself up for grief. *Do not think for a minute* that you can lure a man to coffee with the promise of beauty and then stun into submission with your scintillating personality and your true beauty, which unfortunately lies deep, deep, *deep* beneath the skin.

As illustrated above, there are four basic arenas for lying in a personal ad: age, height, weight, and penis size. How truthful to be is the **Woman-Never-Gives . . . Principle.** You know the one: A woman never gives her age or weight, that kind of thing. There are some areas in which you can fudge, but some in which you should be scrupulously truthful.

Most people are truthful about their age, they'll just say "forty-two (looks thirty-two)," which is acceptable—for some reason, many gay men age better than their straight counterparts; this may be due to our obsession with skin care products, or then again because we tend to collect in cities near those moisturizing and positive ionizing oceans.

It is almost a necessity to lie about your weight; this is the catch-22 of ads. Everybody will assume that you're lying anyway, nobody confesses their real weight unless they're perfectly buff. If you are carrying a few extra pounds at 190, go ahead and say you're 180, as that way when people who read your ad do the necessary ad b.s. math, they will arrive at your actual weight.

Don't lie about your height: Add an inch if you're really insecure, but most people can figure out your exact height the moment they meet you. Weight can be artfully concealed, height cannot.

Penises come in only three sizes in personal ads: 7", 8", and 9". How and why this happened is lost to history. All the same, 7" has come to mean an average penis, 8" to mean nice, and 9" to mean *wow*! None of this has any basis in reality: Pick up a ruler. Put the thumb of one hand on the zero. Put the thumb of the other hand on the nine. *Isn't that scary?* Relax: Almost nobody who claims such equipment really has 9"—it's a gay metaphor for a big one. When you go to describe your penis (which you most certainly don't have to do when writing a relationship ad), just choose one of the three available models.

That takes care of the physical basics. But having acceptable numbers is only the first step toward getting him to call you. You need to write an ad that stands out—just a little. Don't be wacky or kooky or surreal, unless these are personal traits you can't help displaying at all times. *Don't be snippy.* Don't write that you're "a successful quality professional tired of the trash I meet in bars." Maybe you're serious in demanding postgraduate degrees in anyone you meet for coffee, but if you make that clear in the hundred words or less that your ad should run, everybody who reads it will hate you, *including* the men you want to impress and attract. Don't start out by complaining about how hard it is to find someone. Be positive! *This is a list of your assets* you are giving to someone to attract them. Would you write on your résumé "I left this job because my boss was a real mean bitch?" Then don't mention your breakup with your last boyfriend in your ad.

There's a good reason your ad should run under a hundred words—several good reasons, actually. First, it costs less. Second, an ad that runs on and on and on is an ad that gives the reader *too much information* about you. Sketch yourself—don't paint yourself. Giving too much information makes you sound desperate to be understood.

Here's a sample of a successful ad:

GWM, 34, 6'1", 190, br/gr, published novelist, in shape, mostly bottom, urban creature, loves movies, museums, theater, dining out, dancing, female jazz vocals, reading, travel, seeks man 25–40, top, in shape, for good times. Sense of humor essential, modesty preferred over arrogance. Extra points for dark curly hair!

So what makes this a successful ad? It's short enough to be easily digested—remember: Your ad is one of hundreds that he's reading or at least skimming. You want to make an impression quickly; you want to differentiate yourself from the others; and you want to convey exactly what you want.

The list of interests is short and to the point; it tells someone a lot about what kind of person you are: "Urban creature" is a type, and identifying yourself as a type may make you feel unremarkable, but it does give a lot of information about you in two words. It's important to tell him what you're looking for sexually; if you're mostly bottom, say it! You're trying to find what you want, right? Then how can you find it if you don't tell him what you want?

Everyone wants someone with a sense of humor, so that doesn't tell much about you, but "modesty preferred over arrogance" says a lot about you—and what you're looking for. The dark curly hair bit is iffy, frankly: You don't want to make anyone think they can't call if they don't have DCH, but if that's the thing that trips your trigger, well, you'd better put it in.

You may really want a man who's exactly X tall, X old, X-inch waist, etc., but don't write an ad that narrows it down too far; you may end up alienating exactly the man you want with your finicky list. All kinds of men will call your ad, if one is too short or too tall or too old or too young, just don't return the call.

Screening Your Calls: The advantage of placing an ad over answering someone else's is that you're in control. If you have written a good ad and have not demanded a photo (which, if looks are all you're interested in, will save you trouble, but will inconvenience potential respondees and thus make them less likely to reply), chances are that you will get multiple responses. You are not obligated to answer any of them. If you are an excruciatingly nice person, you may feel the need to call everybody back, even the ones you didn't like: *Don't do it.* He'd rather not hear back from you and be able to think you're a jerk than hear back from you and have to listen to your explanation of how he just doesn't do anything for you. Voices tell a lot about people; listen to each response several times before making up your mind whether to delete it or to save it and answer it.

When to Call: Don't call him back the same day he leaves a message for your ad. It makes you seem too eager—and too needy. Wait a day—but not longer than two. After you've actually

talked, of course, feel free to return his calls whenever yo
Just don't jump the first time he barks.

Your First Conversation: Rules Girls will tell you to keep
your first conversation short, as this will make him want you
more. Bosh. The longer your first conversation goes, the better
shot you have at actually getting along when you meet. It helps if
you're the kind of person who likes to talk on the phone, of
course. When the conversation runs out of gas, as even the best
one will, tell him you have to go but this was a nice conversation
and would he like to meet for coffee? This is safe: If he stayed on
the phone with you that long, the answer is almost always going to
be yes.

Your First Date: Do I really have to tell you this? *Meet for coffee, not dinner.* The last thing you want is to find yourself chained
to a table through three courses as someone completely unattractive to you lectures you on How They Figure the Prime Rate.
Rules Girls will tell you that coffee is good because it keeps it
short, and you need to always leave the poor dog wanting more. I
will tell you that coffee is good because it makes for an easy escape should things go horribly wrong—and if things go well, nobody on the coffeehouse staff is going to tell you to move along.

If the date has gone well but it's early, at the end of it say, "This
has been really nice, but I need to get some real food now." This is
his opportunity to say, "Me, too. Maybe we could go get something to eat?" If he doesn't, don't sweat it. You'll see him again;
you can have dinner next time. *Don't ask him to dinner*—it sounds
like you're begging him not to leave.

▼14
The On-Line Principle

This is our last topic under this category. What's that? you say. Why nothing about phone sex? Why, for the same reason there's nothing about how to meet Mr. Right in the back of the dirty-book store: *Because it's not going to happen!* Phone sex lines are full of dissemblers, deceivers, and druggies. You may find yourself making a hot phone sex date with Mr. Right only to find yourself showing up at a nonexistent address, or waiting for someone who never shows up at your house, or, worse, who shows up and spends the next six hours rooting through his tweaker bag looking for that one kind of lube he's just *got* to use. Some of you may very well have had fabulous experiences on phone sex lines—write me and tell me all about it.

Cruising on-line, however, offers the immediate gratification of phone sex without as many of the dangers. Now, some people will try to tell you that people with computers are just more respectable and safer than people who have only phones. Alas, there are just as many crazy people with computers as there are with phones. The difference is the degree of assurance you get cruising on-line. You get to talk to your potential date, and you have a name for him you can pass on to others if he screws you over, and you can exchange photos on the spot. For the purposes of this chapter, we'll limit the discussion to the most popular on-line cruising destination: America Online. Herewith, a tour of AOL you will *never* get in the official manual.

The first thing you need to do is create a secondary account. You don't want to go into the chat rooms as "OOUTLAND;" you don't know who else is in there or how crazy they might be. Create a "hunting name" you can log on as instead. AOL is pretty liberal about these, although a friend's chosen name of "myckyrmth" had to be changed. Like your personal ad, this should be concise and yet give valuable info about you: "SlaveBoy" or "Hottop," for instance, although should you pick something obvious, AOL will tell you it's already taken and ask you if you'd like to be, say, "SlaveBoy2394," which gets you your desired name but indicates your lack of imagination.

The second thing you need to do is create a member profile. Choose the "key word" button from your tool bar; this will take you to your own profile list. *Don't fill in your real name on this form!* This profile is available to anyone who wants to see it. Under "name," write something like "Later" or "Yours gets mine." Read a few other guys' profiles to see how they do it; most use the "hobbies" line to describe themselves and what they're looking for. This is your on-line personal ad; treat it accordingly.

The third thing you need is a picture. Yes, this can be a hassle, not only getting a flattering picture of yourself but getting it scanned at a service bureau. *Do it.* Most guys have pictures and won't meet you without seeing yours. After all, without a photo, it might as well be phone sex, right? If you're not computer literate, tell the guy at the service bureau you need to have the picture saved as a GIF or JPEG file. If you're shy about taking a racy picture to the service bureau (and it doesn't have to be a racy picture, just one that shows your face and the shape of your body), you can wait until you make an on-line friend with a scanner or digital camera who's willing to help you out.

Now you're ready to begin.

People Connection is AOL's live chat area. When you click on the two little faces on your tool bar, you'll be popped into a "lobby." If you just want to chat with anyone who comes along, sit back and enjoy. However, should you want to make a beeline for the men, click on "chat rooms." This will take you to AOL's list of conference rooms. Don't spend your time scrolling through the list on the right of the screen just yet—these are all innocuous conversations that won't get you any men. Instead, click on the button labeled "Member Rooms." Magically, the list of groups like "Sewing Friends" and "Spelling Champs" will be replaced with groups like "M4M Dungeon" and "STR8 But Curious." *This is it, kids.*

You will find that most of the rooms you want to be in are full. If you see that there are twenty-three people in a room, you can double-click on it, but you'll be told the room is full. Here's how to get around that: If you want to get into the room labeled "SanfranciscoM4M" and it's full, click on "Create a Room" and type in, say, "SanfranciscoM4M 2" or 3, or 4, for that matter, if it's evening. Much to your surprise, rather than finding yourself all alone in a new room, you will usually find yourself in a busy room that was out of your sight because it was way down the list of active rooms. You *could* pick the room titled "HoustonM4M" because it's not full even it you're in Sacramento, but the point is to actually make a connection with someone in person, right?

Once you've found a room that's right for your tastes and geographic location, click on that little heart in the upper right corner of your screen—this adds the room to your list of "favorite places," which means you can go back to that room with a single click next time rather than having to go through the lobby.

So you're in a room. *Now what?* On the left side of your screen is the constantly updated chat area. You can type your own comments in or keep your own counsel. On the right side is a list of everyone else in the room. Start out by going through this list: When you enter the room, your name will be on top of the list. Start double-clicking on names beneath yours. A box will appear with the options "Message" and "Get Info." Click on "Get Info" and you'll be whisked to his profile. Should you like what you see, you can close the profile window and click on "message." This is how most people meet on AOL. A window will open: "Send an instant message to Hottop147." Just type "hey" or "hi" or "liked your profile." He will instantly get an open window with your message. Give him a minute to respond—as in, time to find you on the list, double-click you, read your profile, and decide if or how to respond. Of course, as all this is going on, other people are reading your profile, too, and deciding whether or not to send you instant messages (IMs for short on AOL).

If you don't want to approach anyone that directly, you may find yourself sitting in this room, waiting for someone to send you an instant message, and not getting any. In which case, you have two options: If you're too shy or nervous to participate in the conversation, you can bail out and find another room. Or you can start talking and make more of an impression on the others with your repartee than you did with your profile.

However, a well-written profile will sooner or later get you a connection. Leave your instant message window open as the two of you shuttle messages back and forth. You may write him right back and wonder why he isn't writing you back as quickly; remember that some people are more popular than others and have many irons in the fire—he could be juggling several instant message windows at once. If the conversation goes well, sooner or later he will ask you (or you will ask him), "Have you got a GIF?" This is that photo we were talking about earlier.

This is when you need to make certain decisions. If he's got a photo, and you've got a photo, and you agree to trade, no problem. However, if one party has one and the other doesn't, this can get complicated. After all, if you send him yours and he doesn't have one, then he's got a lot more information about what you look like than you have about what he looks like. Whether you want to do this, and go on from there without that information about him, depends on how trusting you are and how important looks are to you. Some guys don't have pictures because it's too complicated; others because they don't like to be judged on their looks, others . . . because they don't photograph well.

The best way to handle your photo is to E-mail it to yourself before you get started cruising on-line. That's partly because it takes so long to upload photos, and you want him to have it ASAP. That way, you can simply forward the mail you sent to yourself to him—which is much faster. It's also partly because you don't want to send him a copy of the message you just sent to someone else—he doesn't want, and shouldn't have, a list of everyone else you've exchanged pictures with. Let him think he's special!

Viewing his photo is easy: Open the mail he sent you and click on "download file." AOL will suggest you save it to a folder called "download" and will offer to name it whatever name he gave his picture, and once you do that, the software will automatically open the file on your screen as well as save it to disk for your future reference.

After you've each gotten a look at the other, it's polite to send another instant message, even if you've decided that you're not interested. *Don't be a jerk.* Remember: He's got friends on-line, and he's got your on-line name. If you've gotten as far as seeing his picture, you've had something resembling a conversation. If you then decide you're not interested, and you don't even reply, it's like being in a bar and walking away from someone in the middle of a sentence. And if you *do* like what you see, well, you know what to do from there.

Cruising on-line is better for finding sex than love. Nonetheless, you will find that if you do it right, you will not only have wonderful conversations that will lead to real dates, but you'll make friends as well. Meeting people is the key to meeting Mr. Right, and if you participate in the conversations as well as cruise the profiles, you'll find yourself seeing familiar names in no time. And who knows when or where he'll come along?

GETTING HIM

▼ 1

The Wallet Principle

So it's happened. At the bar, on-line, in the classroom, at the bookstore, *wherever.* You've been putting yourself out there and you've found yourself in conversation with HIM. He's attractive, he's easygoing, he's got something to say, he's enjoying the conversation. *Keep it that way.* Now, let's be real. Once again, this is life, not Danielle Steel: The first desirable man you hit it off with is probably not going to be the one you end up with. *Be prepared for this.* Think of him as a trial run. I know: It's been just you and the Little Debbie cakes together in your apartment for years now, and the temptation is to *jump him, pin him, and rope him.* Don't even think about it. You've managed to get his attention; the way to keep it is not to let your eyes suddenly and horrifyingly turn into twin whirlpools of need. DO NOT LET HIM KNOW how very attractive you find him.

This is the **Wallet Principle:** If you were walking down the street and saw a wallet bulging with cash sitting there on the sidewalk, would you casually bend down to tie your shoe and scoop it up, or would you jump up and down, shouting, "A wallet! I found a wallet full of cash!" So why wouldn't you behave the same way when you find a desirable man?

This is your next lesson: *Men are not attracted to need.* The worst thing you can do is display your Flaming Volcano of Need. Men want to see what you have, not what you lack. This is often not easy, especially when you find someone who seems to have it all. "You're so great!" you can't help gushing. "You're so beautiful!" If he's that good-looking, *he's heard it before*! You might as well natter on about the weather for all the impression you're making on him. Reminding him of how much he has on a regular basis makes him feel that he's got more than you, and that makes him think you are beneath him on the Food Chain. It also classes you with all the other men who've said the same boring thing to him before, *all the other men he is no longer dating*. Wait until he makes some self-deprecating comment and say lightly, "That's ridiculous. You're incredibly attractive—you know that!" It will startle him—he will turn and look at you. You will have said something different from what the others have said, and that will make you different from *them*. *Trust me* on this one. Sure, men need compliments as much as women do (who knows, maybe more, since we get so few), but showing him, *not* telling him, that you're interested in him and happy to be spending time with him is far more attractive and effective than drooling.

In this section I will discuss some real-life incidents to illustrate my points. Here's a case study of a first date that went horribly wrong: Steven S. and George L. talked on the phone after George answered Steven's ad. Their conversation went well; they had a lot in common, were around the same age, both had successful careers. They met for coffee; George showed up not expecting much and was pleasantly surprised, while Steven went in full of nerves he managed to keep down only with his antianxiety medication. After half an hour they decided to meet again for a real date. George left the date with a sense of pleasant anticipation; Steven, however, went manic immediately afterward. "At last!" he crowed to friends. "I've found HIM! I just know this is it!" Steven spent many of his waking hours after his date distractedly writing his date's last name after his own and wondering if there was enough space in his current apartment for two or if he and George would have to move into a bigger place.

When they met for their first real date, George found to his consternation that Steven was not only excited but overeager. To his every idle comment, Steven would say, "We are so alike!" or "We have so much in common." Steven wouldn't stop thanking George for going out with him, and asked him if he'd had a lover before, why it ended, and other personal information best left asked later in a relationship. Steven stared at George over the dinner table so intently that his Flaming Volcano of Need made a mess all over the table.

Needless to say, when Steven sent George flowers the next day, George called Steven, thanked him for the flowers, and said that he was very busy just then but that he would call Steven in a few weeks . . . *if he had time.* A grieving Steven asked his friends, "What did I do wrong?"

Chances are, if you're that needy, you're not ready for a relationship. You're expecting something from it that it can't give you. *You're expecting a man to make it all better.* If you are that needy, and you want to ignore me and try to use a man to make it all better anyway, remember what Steven did wrong (that should be obvious) and *play it cool* next time.

2

The Leave-Food-on-the-Plate Principle

There are two ways you're going to meet a man. Either you're going to meet him the way straight people meet—at a business function, in a class, in the bookstore—or the way gay people often (not always) meet, i.e., you may be intimately acquainted with many of his body parts before you even know his name. Each situation requires a different approach if you're to see him again. Let's start with the nonsexual encounter.

So you're having a nice conversation, you've got a firm cap on your Flaming Volcano of Need, and then the conversation runs out of gas, as it always does eventually. "Well . . ." you say, and *leave it at that.* Give *him* the opportunity to ask *you* out.

This is the **Leave-Food-on-the-Plate Principle:** Many diet books will advise you not to eat compulsively everything in front of you—to *deliberately not clean your plate.* It's about avoiding compulsion; in this case, the compulsion to do everything you think you can to get him to go out with you, including asking him first. If he's interested, he'll propose something—lunch, a study date, a movie. If he's vague, as in "We should get together sometime," agree: "Yeah, that would be great." This is one of the places the Rules Girls know whereof they speak. Men like a challenge—they like to hunt and pursue. *Let him ask for your phone number.* Oh, you can offer it readily, but he probably won't call it. If nothing happens and it's time to either go or offer your number, *don't* *do it!* If you've met socially, chances are you'll meet again. Let him spend some time kicking himself, feeling like he blew it because he didn't ask you out: That way, next time he sees you, he won't waste another chance.

Don't feel obligated to have sex on the first date. In fact, it's a good idea if you don't. Let's face it: Sex on the first date often equals a one-night stand. However, if he finds himself not having sex on the second or even third dates, as "The Rules" suggests for women, you might be asking for trouble. After all, for gay men, sex is an extremely important part of relationships. Sure, you want to know what else you have in common, but if the sex is no good, well . . . It's often best to find out if that part of the relationship is going to fly or not before you spend too much time with Mr. Wrong.

3

The Sharon Stone Principle

Now, we've trashed "The Rules" pretty good, but let's face it: There are definitely times where Rules Girls know whereof they speak. You don't want to give this guy everything he wants as soon as he asks for it. In addition to hiding your Flaming Volcano of Need, and leaving food on the plate, it's important to practice the **Sharon Stone Principle:** Have you ever seen a Sharon Stone movie in which she fell all over a guy? I mean, sure, once he's seduced her, but doesn't she treat him a little like meat for a while first?

This book advocates honesty—for the most part. But there are times when honesty is not the best policy. *Don't* volunteer the information that you're looking for a mate; *don't* ask him if he's looking for one. And if he asks, tell him you're seeing a few people, none of them seriously, and you suppose you might get serious about somebody someday, but that it's not happening right now. Believe me: He will *immediately* begin trying to become the somebody who can impress you. Men love Sharon Stone because Sharon Stone doesn't give a damn if they do or not!

This is going beyond capping your FVON. This is about showing yourself as someone who doesn't *need* a man. Because here's the next secret about men: They want to be needed! Now, wait a minute, you say: But you told me to hide my need! Absolutely: He wants you to need *him*, not "a man." If you show your generalized need the minute you meet him, well, then, you're saying any warm body will do and would he like to fill the position? Of course not! He wants you to get to know *him* and find *him* indispensable.

This is why Rules Girls tell you to tell him that you're busy, that you *might* be able to squeeze him in, that the competition for you is pretty intense, that you, *like Sharon Stone,* don't need to chase any man when you've got so many chasing you. Is it a lie? Sure it is, sometimes. But the fact of the matter is, it's a lie that becomes true the more you say it: The more you tell men you don't need them, the less you will need them! And the more likely you will be to find your equal, and someone you can really build a relationship with that will last.

4

The Last Tango Principle

Now, let's say you met him at a sex club, a bathhouse, or a bar, and ended up doing it with only minimal information about him as a person. But let's say the sex was GREAT. I don't mean: Gee, that was nice. I mean: *The paint peeled off the walls.* Listen: *Men want passion.* They want hot sex, and lots of it. You may say to yourself that you're willing to sacrifice sexual satisfaction in order to get a relationship, and you may even find yourself saying it out loud at some point and hearing him agree with you. *Bosh.* If you don't end up cheating, he will. You're a man: Accept it.

This is the **Last Tango Principle,** as in *Last Tango in Paris:* Sooner or later, you'll meet someone and it'll happen: peeling paint, scorched sheets, the cat in hiding for three days afterward. That's when you'll know he's the man for you.

So what do you do now? You're in the grip of your male animal nature; you've GOT to have this guy again. And again. After sex like that, it's completely acceptable to deliver a compliment. "That was great. You're an incredibly good [whatever he just did to you]!" If he returns the compliment, and means it (you'll know if he does—look him in the eye when he says it; if he's not looking you in the eye, he's thinking about somebody else), you've got a chance. But you're still in dangerous waters. Men being the dogs they are, and sexual haunts being the purveyors of zipless fun they are, he may very well be the man from the previous paragraph, out tricking out of boredom with his passionless relationship. You need to find out if he's single without hinting that you're looking to rope him. *Be prepared for the worst.* Don't assume his availability. With any luck, he'll ask you a seemingly innocuous question. In my town, San Francisco, the question is: "So, do you live in the city?" If he wants to know that, congratulations. You cannot only answer it, but say, "Yeah, and you?"

Now, the rules are a little different here from what they are with someone you haven't just had sex with. Feel free to make a suggestion: "I'd love to do this again sometime." If he'd love to do it again sometime, too, he'll let you know it. If he didn't have as good a time as you, well, then he isn't the one. Again, like the first guy you have a great conversation with, don't assume the first guy you peel paint with is going to be your new husband. And the same rule still applies: *Take his number, or let him ask for yours— don't offer him your number!*

If you do get to see him again, don't expect to turn him away at the end of your first real date with a kiss. After all, there's no point in playing hard to get when you've already been had. Your relationship started with sex, and that sex is a big part of why you're seeing each other again. Enjoy it.

▼5
The Big A

"The Rules" advises you to hold back little facts about yourself until the relationship is in full swing—things like, "I'm an alcoholic" or "I have horrible scars" or "I'm on Prozac." But HIV is one of those things that you can't just toss off later in the relationship. You've read the ads: You know that some guys are simply not interested in dating someone with HIV. If you're HIV positive and he's phobic about it and is going to reject you when he finds out, you're wasting every second you spend with him anyway. *Positive or negative, talk about it right away.* You know it, he knows it— it's a life-and-death subject. You can wait to tell him you're a compulsive gambling, alcoholic, drug-addicted Whitney Houston fan, but don't wait on this one. You'll earn plenty of brownie points for being honest right from the start. End of lecture.

▼6

The "If You Really Love Me . . ." Principle

Okay: Let's say you've met someone. Within a few dates you're sure that he's everything you could ever want in a man. He's swept you off your feet, you've already had hot, passionate sex, and you're floating on a cloud every minute of the day. So one night, you're getting hot and heavy, and he says, "Let's do it without rubbers. I'm negative!" You, overwhelmed by his wonderfulness and afraid to lose him, either believe him or don't care, because you'd do just about anything he'd ask you to right now.

SCREEEEECCCCHHHH! That's the sound of the brakes you should be putting on *right now.* You may think that he's just as eager as you are to make the complete connection, but if you've known him only a short while, then he's just using you. Listen: You don't *really* know this guy that well. He could be lying; he may sound convincing, but then, maybe he's lied to himself so often, he believes it himself. If you're negative, think of the last time you had unsafe sex—remember the fear, the anxiety, the guilt? Are you really so desperate to please this guy you just met that you're willing to go through that for the six months it takes for an infection to show up on the tests?

Unsafe sex is one of the hottest topics right now in our community; many longtime lovers are riding bareback when both partners have stayed negative and monogamous, and one day you and he may decide to do that. You may think you'll never really connect with him until you do it bareback, but it takes more than sex without a rubber to really connect with someone. It takes time to build *real trust,* which is what you'd damn well better have before you jump that fence.

The *Stella Dallas* Principle

Once again, as a gay man, it's incumbent on you to remember the lessons Hollywood has taught you. Let's assume you meet the man of your dreams, he sweeps you off your feet, you have window-rattling sex, and the drift of the conversation allows you to ask if he's single. "Oh," he says, "I have a roommate who's sort of my boyfriend, but we don't have anything in common; we don't have the same friends," etc. *RUN RIGHT NOW!* What he means is that he's got a live-in lover, probably of several years standing, and he's tricking out on him. One of the most important skills you can develop is translating what men say into English; the English translation of the above sentence is: "My wife doesn't understand me."

This is the *Stella Dallas* **Principle:** *You do not want to become somebody's mistress.* Think back to any Barbara Stanwyck movie you ever saw. Did the husband ever leave the wife for the mistress? Your chances of winning the lottery are greater than your chances of getting him out of his relationship. Chances are he's quite happy with every aspect of it but the passion, and if he can bonk your brains out and still go home to a clean house and a hearty meal, he'll do it for as long as you let him. I know: Sometimes waiting for your own man gets to be a major drag; a little piece of somebody who seems so right for you can start to look better than nothing at all. But as long as you cling to that little piece, you're out of circulation—*out of the competition.* And that means you'll never get someone who belongs entirely to you. Your goal is to find your own Mr. Right, not to take somebody else's table scraps.

▼8
The Closet-Case Principle

Falling for a gay man who's already in a relationship with another man is bad enough. But if you think *that's* a life of skulking and scuttling, furtive encounters with little or no notice, and a general assault on your self-esteem, try having an affair with a man who hasn't even come to terms with his sexuality yet. On the other hand—don't try it.

Many of the men you meet in sex-only establishments are deeply closeted; some are married (yes, as in, to a woman); some haven't even admitted to themselves, let alone anyone else, that they're gay. (You've heard it: "I'm straight. I'm just doing this to get off"—as if finding a willing woman was *that* hard for a good-looking guy.) Your gay adulterous lover may not hold your hand in public for fear one of his lover's friends will see the two of you together, but your "straight" lover won't even be seen with you near a gay neighborhood, let alone a gay bar. Worst of all, you won't even have to translate when he says his wife doesn't understand him.

There are some men who are professionally closeted—that is, their friends know they're gay, their family might even know it, but their coworkers don't. This is generally not pretty—especially because it's not really necessary anymore in the modern urban workplace.

Unless, that is, he happens to be in the armed forces, where his sexuality is still enough in and of itself to get him tossed out. There are a lot of wonderful, well-adjusted men who keep their sexuality a secret because they want to make a career of serving their country, and can't if anyone knows who they sleep with. (How quaint that will sound in a hundred years!) If you meet such a man, you may decide he's worth the secrecy, the lies, the masquerading . . . and I wish you the best. It's a gamble, of course, for the both of you, but if it's love, and the masquerade is about Jesse Helms's dysfunctionality and not your beloved's, it's a whole different ball of wax. Just remember what Mark Twain said—it's much easier to tell the truth than to lie, because that way you don't have to remember what you said last time. Even in a strong, healthy relationship, that kind of secrecy takes its toll.

▼9

The *Fatal Attraction* Principle

As mentioned briefly above in the sex club etiquette section, it's important to remember that your romantic career will not consist solely of endlessly lonely nights that finally end one enchanted evening with the advent of HIM. You are going to go on a lot of first dates. You are going to reject a lot of these guys, and a lot of these guys are going to reject you. It is important to remember the *Fatal Attraction* **Principal:** If he's going, let him go. Boiling a bunny in his stockpot will probably lead only to your own gruesome death.

There's an etiquette to rejecting someone, and an etiquette to taking rejection gracefully. Most of us know how to reject someone without being a bastard: "I'm really busy with work these days" or "I'm not looking for a relationship right now" or "I lost it in the war" (just seeing if you're paying attention).

But how to accept rejection gracefully? You want to believe him when he says he's really busy, don't you? So you press: You say, "Well, maybe some weekend you might have a free afternoon we could meet for coffee?" DON'T DO IT! You'll only be leaving a bad taste in both your mouths at the end of what is probably your last conversation ever. *Of course* if he's really *that* busy and he has a free afternoon, he's going to spend that time with friends, or resting, or looking for sex with someone who is *not you.*

The fact of the matter is, *men make time for what they want.* If he says he doesn't have time, or he's really busy, or whatever the excuse is, just look at him as if you believe him, and say, "Well, thank you for meeting me, and good luck." You can't press a man to want what he doesn't want, and going Glenn Close on him is not going to get him. Don't ask him what it was you did wrong, or don't have, or if it was your breath. If you must know, try and recount the experience exactly as it happened to a good friend, who will be honest with you and tell you if he can figure it out.

Now, sometimes he *really, really is* that busy (this happens mostly in New York City), and he just may call you. But whatever you do, don't sit by the phone waiting for the call—write it off as another losing lottery ticket, and go out and try again.

▼10

The Eggs-in-One-Basket Principle

This one's short and sweet: Don't put all your eggs in one basket! Sure, it's taken a long time to find someone you want to see more than a couple times. However, this does *not* mean you can stop dating other guys. If you stop dating other guys, the next thing you know you'll be planning the wedding with this one way too early.

There are three reasons to keep dating other men. The first and most important is your mental health: You need to avoid the trap of pushing a relationship too fast. It's easier to hold yourself back from rushing things if you've got more than one iron in the fire.

The second is insurance: What if you stop dating everyone but this one guy, and he suddenly disappears? You may be sure as sure can be that he'd never dump you, but what if he gets transferred? Gets hit by a bus? Joins a cult? Gets back together with his old boyfriend, whom he never really got over?

The third is a little bit of Rules Girls psychology that works—a little devious, like all Rules Girls methods, but deviousness in small doses isn't such a bad thing. Namely, you want to remind him that *you don't need him.* Remember the Sharon Stone Principle? Men are competitive: If he's reminded every now and then that he's not the only one you're seeing, it'll keep him on his toes; it also tells him you're someone worth having—and that he's someone worth having, too: After all, if there are other guys who are after you, it's not like you're taking him because you're desperate.

The Donna Reed Principle

You've heard it: "The way to a man's heart is through his stomach." *How true*. In the long run, you will find that spending as much time with *The Joy of Cooking* as you spent with *The Joy of Gay Sex* will not be in vain.

This is the **Donna Reed Principle:** Showing him the domestic comforts he can expect should he mate with you is crucial (at the right moment; more on that in a minute). From time immemorial, nothing has so delighted a man as sitting down at a table and having food magically appear. And if you can present not just "food," but a meal to make him weep for his dear sainted mother, well . . .

Of course there's a danger that he might expect you to devote the rest of your life to cooking suppers to rival Scheherazade's stories, so you should make it clear from the first that while you love to cook, you are much too busy to do it every day (unless you're a professional chef, in which case you may be stuck).

Clean up your room! Sure, you live like a bachelor, with clothes on the floor and bits of paper and bills scattered around. "After all," you say, "nobody's going to see it but me." With that attitude, nobody ever *will* see it, or if he does, he won't stay for long. Believe me, he may be just as much of a pig as you are, but he's going to judge *you* harshly for it. It's just how men are.

Sure, you can get away with it if you're a lean, cool, slouching twenty-four-year-old, constantly pushing your long, glossy dark hair out of your sullen, beautiful face . . . but if that's you, you're reading this book only to laugh at those of us who have to work a little harder to catch a man. Get outta here!

Your house should *always* be clean. Who knows when you'll meet him? What if he asks if he can come up for a drink of water? Play the Barbie Game: Think about your dream house, just you and Ken all snuggled up inside. What's Barbie's secret? She's got lots of closet space, and she hangs up everything, from her prom dress to her astronaut suit.

However, there is a dark side to this principle. You can scare a man off if you thrust your domestic accomplishments in his face too quickly. *No man wants to be caught!* You don't want him thinking you're planning to rope him into domesticity; instead, you want to introduce your domestic talents gradually. Let him see your clean apartment anytime, but I wouldn't cook him dinner until after at least six or eight dates, and even then, only if you end up casually introducing the subject, as in "I was in the Yuppie Market the other day picking up some seafood for my cioppino, when . . ." which allows him to ask, "Oh, do you like to cook?" *Of course you do.* (If you really, really hate to cook, accept that you're going to have to develop other talents to make up for this deficit.)

Introduce him subtly to the domestic joys that await him; let these marvelous qualities of yours settle to the bottom of his subconscious, which is where most men make up their minds about affairs of the heart anyway. This doesn't mean waiting on him hand and foot, of course, only that you're both eager to please, and capable of pleasing, and not just in the bedroom.

▼12

When to Meet the Friends (His and Yours)

So you're dating someone now. The sex is good, the conversation rarely flags, you do fun stuff together. Of course you think he's everything but the kitchen sink, but then, you are probably at least partially blinded by lust at this point in the relationship (if you're lucky). A little objectivity is in order, and you are in no position to provide it. The best way to get it is to meet each other's friends.

His meeting your friends will give them the opportunity to either shore up your decision or say, "What the hell are you doing?" Your meeting his friends will give you the opportunity to meet people who are like your sweetie but who are not your sweetie. Nothing tells you more about someone than who their friends are. If he's been keeping a secret life from you, this is when you'll find out.

A case study: Roger E. and Gene S. were going out. Roger was the quiet, stay-at-home type, despite his astonishing good looks. Gene was so smitten with Roger that he told him that he, too, preferred quiet evenings at home . . . well, at least as long as they were evenings with Roger. Roger and Gene got to the point in their relationship where it was important to meet each other's friends. All of Roger's friends liked Gene; he really seemed like the guy Roger had been looking for all this time.

But then Roger met Gene's friends, all of whom were party animals to the core and who enjoyed regaling Roger with Gene's legendary exploits at the last White Party. Roger turned disbelievingly to Gene, who said, "That's who I used to be! I like my life with you now." Roger believed him because he wanted to, but six months later, as the volcanic passion that had fueled the relationship so far started to fade, Gene was back on the circuit and Roger was left alone in tears.

This is not to say that a leopard can't change his spots, only that some people will say and do things to get what they want even if they know they're lying. Meeting his friends will tell you if he's on the level when he talks about the life he leads.

The Cosmo Girl Principle

That's enough about his friends. What about your own? You *have* seen them lately, haven't you? Okay, you've met them for lunch . . . called them . . . ?

As stated long ago by the expert in this whole field, Ms. Helen Gurley Brown herself, the **Cosmo Girl Principle** is simple: You don't abandon your friends just because *he*'s come along to make it all better. I know how it goes: You meet him on Friday, spend the whole weekend with him, and then he calls you at work Monday afternoon—what are you doing tonight?

Let me tell you the story of Adam B. Adam met Robert A. one fine day just after moving to a new city. Their relationship was pure fireworks from the start. They found themselves literally unable to keep their hands off each other. Work was the only thing that kept them apart. Adam and Robert spent every night together for a year—yes, *every night* for a year. A true story.

But by the end of that year, Adam and Robert had realized that their scratch 'n' screw relationship wasn't good for either of them, and they broke up. And so here was Adam, having lived in a new city for a year, without a single friend outside work because he'd become dependent on Robert for all his socializing. Adam made friends quickly once he got to work on it, but it was rough going for a while.

Your friends will be with you always; your lovers quite often come and go. Friends will forgive you for dropping off their radar during the first heat of passion, but if you're a good friend, you'll come up for air every now and then. This is both for your mental health and your sense of decency.

▼14
The Hugh Grant Principle

So everything has been going swimmingly. You've been dating for . . . oh, let's say six months. You've met each other's friends, and that's gone well. You've been away for at least one weekend together, and that's gone well. You go thrift-shopping together on weekends, or Roller-blading, or what*ever*. The sex is *still* great; in fact, it's getting better. You look back at your life before him and wonder, *How did I ever survive without him?* If you have nodded yes to all of these statements, unless you have some kind of emotional deficiency, you are probably in love.

There's just one problem: *You're deathly afraid to tell him.*

And why shouldn't you be? There's the possibility that he doesn't love you back, that you'd scare him off because the "L" word usually prefaces the "C" word (commitment) which leads to the "M" word, or maybe even because you're scared of commitment yourself—after all, you're a man, too, and giving up all the other potentially more wonderful men out there for the one you have is never easy.

Every relationship eventually runs into the **Hugh Grant Principle:** In *Four Weddings and a Funeral,* Hughie has to tell Andie MacDowell that he loves her, or he'll lose her. It's the *last* thing he wants to say, but he knows what will happen if he doesn't.

Sooner or later you're going to have to say it, too: It's a fact, it's what you feel, and you've got to share your feelings with someone if the relationship is to continue.

You really should wait until you've been dating awhile. Don't be lured in by the fact that gay time is different from straight time. Yes, three dates between two men happens as often as nine dates between a man and a woman; nonetheless, to get to know another person well enough to really know if you love him *takes time,* whether you're straight or not. Six months is about right.

When and how to tell him: Don't tell him while you're lying on the couch watching TV. *Don't* tell him right before he goes to work. Plan it ahead of time; try to make it a romantic occasion without being sappy—i.e., suggest a drive out to the ocean in the early evening, or a walk in the woods, somewhere beautiful, where you won't be surrounded by other people. Don't get down on your knees; it's cliché. The last thing you want him to do when you declare your love is laugh. Here's a sample speech you might modify so it sounds natural coming out of your own mouth:

"You know, we've been dating about six months now, and I think we've both been having a really great time. [With any luck he will concur here.] I've forgotten what it was like before I met you—I mean, I can't imagine going back to that life. You've really become an incredibly important person in my life. I've thought about it a lot, and I've been waiting to say this until I was sure, but . . . I'm in love with you. I love you."

It's all right to stumble a bit—I would hope that you would, in fact. If it comes out too easily, chances are you don't mean it.

Of course, *this is the most dangerous moment of your life.* Which is why you're nervous. What if he doesn't love you back? Or, worse, feels obligated to say he loves you when he doesn't? You might want to add to your speech—after a minute to see his reaction—that you don't need him to say it right now himself if he doesn't feel it yet. *Don't jump in the ocean* if he doesn't say it back right away. He may need time to process his own feelings; maybe he's just been coasting along, having a good time, without really thinking about it, whereas you've been thinking about it all along. If three months pass without an identical declaration from him, and you can't handle a relationship that doesn't include his feeling the same thing for you, you might want to start thinking about moving on.

▼15

The Miss Havisham Principle

While you may need to move on if he goes past the ninety-day limit after your own declaration of love, it's equally important not to jump the gun. Don't go into every relationship wondering if this is IT. You may find yourself dating someone for six months, a year, maybe even longer, without it really turning into True Love. And yet you may find yourself pretty happy with what you've got—a nice guy, good times, a warm body in your bed on Sunday morning. Hey: It's a lot more than some people have.

The **Miss Havisham Principle** is based on that old dear from Dickens's *Great Expectations*. Come on, think back. They made you read it in high school: Miss Havisham, still sitting there in her wedding dress with her wedding cake mostly eaten by rats, many, many years after being left at the altar. The **Miss Havisham Principle** states, simply, "Don't plan the wedding." Accept the fact that most relationships, even good ones, don't end up at the altar. Don't make final statements like "This is the guy I want to spend the rest of my life with" if you've spent only three months with him. Yes, it's all very soft and fluffy and New Age to say, "Let it flow," but, buddy, that's what you gotta do.

Give it plenty of time before you start thinking about moving in together. The best thing you can do is date someone for a year—yes, a whole year—before you make any decisions about living together. It's enough time to see not only whether he leaves the cap off the toothpaste, but how he treats other people, how he treats you, what kind of life you'd have with him if you lived with him. Ease into it: spending your weekends together, taking trips together, spending *progressively* more time together until you're sure you want this guy underfoot all the time.

▼16

The "Let's Be Friends" Principle

You may find yourself dating someone for a while, things going on pretty well as far as you're concerned. Okay, maybe there's no great passion, but there are a lot of things about this guy that really attract you—you've got a lot in common, you can talk for hours without the conversation flagging, maybe even sit in silence and not feel awkward. But then one day to your enormous surprise he tells you he's not interested in pursuing the relationship anymore, but "can we be friends?"

Now, straight guys treat this as the kiss of death. For them, men are friends and women are lovers. To them, this doesn't really register as an offer of friendship, only as a brush-off, the sort of late-in-the-game version of "I'm really busy these days; I'll call you." But again, the rules are different for gay men. We have a lot more sex than they do, and we meet a lot more people via sex than they do. Many are the close friendships between gay men that developed between two people who were attracted to each other for various reasons, had sex, found it didn't work, and became friends.

If this guy really does have a lot of qualities that you like but the passion is the only thing that's missing—take him at his word! He probably feels the same connection to you that you feel to him; unlike women, men don't keep dating someone they don't like to "give them a chance to show their true colors." If he's dated you this long, he likes you, too. Don't let yourself see this as some kind of blow to your self-esteem, don't run away from him embarrassed because he didn't want you as a lover. Here's a "Rule" for you to remember: If there's anything harder to find than Mr. Right, it's a good, true friend. *Never* pass up an opportunity to make one of those!

KEEPING
HIM

▼1

The Big Difference

Here's the big difference between you and a Rules Girl: For Rules Girls, the object is getting married. *The Rules* ends like a Victorian novel, with the reader and her beloved tied in holy matrimony. Now, until the Supreme Court finally gets around to voting 6–3 to overturn the "Defense of Marriage" Act, no clever strategizing on your part is going to get his ring on your finger. With no community property laws to bind two people, gay relationships are simply easier to break up than straight marriages. It's going to require a lot more than a piece of paper to keep your relationship alive.

If you've been following my advice, you've met someone with whom you share interests, activities, and great sex. Keeping all these things going is the key to keeping your relationship.

The Warren Beatty Principle

Okay: So you've been dating him for a good long while—maybe not a year, but long enough to think, he could be The One. You're ready to get serious; he seems pretty taken with you. There's just one problem: When the two of you started dating, you were both seeing a few other people. (Remember the Eggs-in-One-Basket Principle?) Now, gradually, you've washed those other men right out of your hair. The problem is, he's still roving a bit. Maybe you can live with an open marriage (see the next principle), but few marriages work that *start* as open relationships. If there isn't enough singular passion between you and him to keep him interested solely in you for at least a few years, well, maybe you haven't found the right guy.

But let's say you're holding on to this guy—and not because you're needy. Let's say he's got all the qualities you want in a man except the ability to commit. That's right: It's the same problem straight guys have, only worse. See, women are in it together to make sure that straight men commit, but we gay men haven't gotten it together like our female counterparts—partly because we've got a culture that makes it so easy to tomcat around, and a lot of us like to know that option is out there. When women want men to behave, they withhold sex; try withholding sex from *your* boyfriend and see how fast he gets it somewhere else!

It's time for a little reverse psychology. He wants to keep his options open; if he meets a Falcon porn star, he wants to be able to drop everything and do him. At the same time, he expects you to keep the home fires burning. Forget it! It's time for you to start dating again. Not with an eye to replacing him, but to remind him what it was like when the two of you first met, and you were a prize to be won, not a trophy to be hung up and forgotten.

This is the **Warren Beatty Principle:** If he wants to keep tom-catting around, you have to remind him that what's good for the goose is good for the . . . well, you're a goose, too, aren't you? Nine times out of ten, if he's not willing to commit, it's because he's taking you for granted. Imagine his surprise when he calls you to set up your usual Friday night date only to discover you have other plans, and not with friends! If he expresses astonishment, remind him gently that he's the one who thought an open relationship was such a good idea. *Men are possessive!* If he really wants you, he'll do what it takes to possess you again. You see, sometimes the best way to interfere with his habits is to make no move to stop him.

Now, despite your best efforts in this department, he may be set in his ways, and you may decide that you can live with his outside interests and take the next step anyway. There are some people for whom open relationships work just fine; both partners are ex-tremely sexual beings, and sometimes one or both work in a bar or in a business in the gay ghetto that provides limitless sexual op-portunities. They have a powerful attraction to each other, as well as the other shared interests that brought them together, but nei-ther of them will ever be happy with one sex partner. Asking them to be monogamous would be like asking a diabetic to work in an ice cream parlor.

But that's usually not the way it works. Instead, one partner says, "I want an open relationship," and the other says, "Okay"— not because it's okay, but because he's afraid of losing his new love. But as time goes by, and he discovers to his horror that his partner *really meant it* when he said he was going to have sex with other men, his rage and jealousy become unmanageable. *Be very sure* that you're going to be okay with this kind of relationship be-fore you consent.

For a lot of couples, the way to keep the relationship together sexually is to expand into three-ways. This gives both partners the thrill of a new man without excluding the other partner from the fun. If this works for you, great. But it's a mathematical law that most of the time, in any three-way, there are two who get really hot for each other and one who gets left out. And if the same partner is getting left out in every three-way, well, trouble's gonna be a-brewin'.

Sooner or later you're going to find in your relationship that the sex dries up. It's just the way of men to tend to lose interest in sex with the same partner; our genetic blueprint urges us to spread our seed as far and wide as possible. Eventually, you're probably going to have to have an open relationship, once it's clear that you are no longer satisfying each other sexually.

The key to keeping the relationship going past that point, then, is to keep the sex as hot as possible for as long as possible, so that by the time it does dry up, you've built a relationship that's not dependent just on the sex for its continued existence, but on the other things you have going together. If sex is something that he's having with you *and* every other hot guy he meets, then you're probably not going to share that passion long enough for other things to cement the relationship.

3

The *Odd Couple* Principle

So you're ready to move in together. Congratulations! You've practiced the **Donna Reed Principle** and kept a neat and tidy home, and now you're well prepared to make a nest with Mr. Right. No matter that he himself is an inveterate slob, right? And while your Southwestern chic decor may suffer a bit from the addition of his chrome and glass furniture, accommodation is what love is all about, right? You won't mind putting the cap back on the toothpaste every morning, or doing all the dishes, or picking his underwear up off the floor. Nor will you mind that his entire wardrobe consists of jeans and T-shirts; you're not ashamed to take him to your favorite swanky restaurant just as he is. . . .

Wrong! The watchword for a successful move-in is *compatibility*. I'll say it again: Opposites attract, but composites connect. While you may think at first that throwing over your whole lifestyle to accommodate him will be a breeze, think back to the **Warren Beatty Principle:** You know perfectly well that you shouldn't commit to an open relationship if that's not really what you want. Accommodation is *not* what love is all about; *compromise* is what love is all about. You may agree that he can put the sling in the guest bedroom, if he agrees not to leave his chaps on the floor every night.

Different tastes and styles don't mean you can't live together; it does mean you have to make a plan *before* you move in together for how you're going to bring your different styles into alignment.

▼4

The Cheatin' Heart Principle

Many relationships start out wonderful and go downhill. But usually these are the kinds of relationships in which both partners are projecting an ideal person onto the other, actual person. And the more you get to know him, the more you realize he's got little irritating habits and crackpot superstitions and bizarre political beliefs. You have to accept that other people have their foibles, and live with them.

And you have to accept that other people make mistakes. Sometimes, these mistakes can take the form of actions taken behind your back. Sometimes, that means he goes out and spends several thousand dollars that you were hoping would go toward his half of a fabulous vacation. Sometimes, it takes the form of sex with a stranger—maybe even sleeping with someone you know.

Now, there's a part of every one of us that wants to figuratively if not literally go home to Mother when this kind of thing happens. And undoubtedly sleeping with one of your friends is not the same as leaving the cap off the toothpaste; nonetheless, you have to ask yourself: Could this have happened to me in the same circumstances? As a man yourself, you know how easy it can be to be led around by your . . . libido. The **Cheatin' Heart Principle** is simple: Put yourself in his shoes before you decide to walk away. Of course, if the two of you have committed for whatever reasons to monogamy and he pulls this again, well, fool me once, shame on you; fool me twice, shame on me.

What is it you need from this guy? Is his undivided sexual attention the most important thing in your relationship? Or are there other things keeping you together, things that are important enough to you to allow you to forgive sexual peccadillos? Think about it.

5

The Marabel Morgan Principle

If you are under the age of thirty, you don't remember old Marabel. But her book *The Total Woman* was to the late seventies what *The Rules* is to the nineties. Marabel basically taught that the secret to keeping a man was keeping him interested. *How right she was.* The **Marabel Morgan Principle** is simple: When the man loses interest in sex with you, it's the first step to losing interest in you, especially if that happens before other things you have in common can cement the relationship.

Now, the problem with Marabel is the same one we gay guys have with "The Rules:" follow it literally by, say, greeting your mate in a piece of slinky lingerie with a rose between your teeth, and he's more likely to be concerned about your heretofore unknown transvestite proclivities than he is to be sexually excited (though you never know). You will have to improvise.

Keeping your sex life charged up is a tricky business. Marabel knew that the element of surprise is important. *Don't* sit on the couch reading *The Joy of Gay Sex;* this implies that there's something wrong with your current sex, which implies that there's something wrong with him, which is going to have the opposite effect from the one you're looking for. *Don't* suggest renting a Falcon film; however, should you be in the video store, you might linger in the adult section until he finds you with the latest Ken Ryker vehicle in your hands, and see what he says. *Don't* reach

under the bed and pull out a sex toy not modeled on anything re-
motely human and wave it in his face without warning.

The trick is to figure out what he likes but hasn't asked for—I
know, I know, it's like asking you to read his mind. Still, every
man has a secret fantasy—more than one, if he's normal. You
don't want him to pull his ultimate fantasy out of the bag until
later in the relationship, unless you want him to blow his psychic
wad all at once. What you can do is improvise—put your tongue
somewhere it hasn't been before, say, and see how he likes it.
Unlike women, who'll put up with doing little things they don't
like that much, most men will tell you if it feels good or not right
away.

Be adventurous. Don't do anything you're not comfortable
doing . . . but you may find that with the right person you'd do
things you'd never dreamed of before. You see, when he goes out
and meets some other guy, he may get excited because he doesn't
know what to expect; but if he also never quite knows what to expect from *you* . . .

Part of keeping the relationship exciting is keeping yourself exciting. *Don't think you can let yourself go* just because you've
moved in with him. Every pound you add around the middle is a
month you can slice off the duration of the exciting part of your
relationship. Rules Girls may think that getting to the altar is the
end of the game, but Marabel knew better. The hard work *never*
ends—sorry, but it's a fact. He may *say* he loves you just the way
you are, he may *say* he doesn't mind those few extra pounds, but
the fact is, one day he's going to meet someone who looks the way
you *used* to look, at which point you can kiss the hot part of your
relationship good-bye. The best thing you can do to keep your relationship hot is to make yourself *more* attractive to him as time
goes by. Work out, dress up, keep up appearances! If he finds that
you get better-looking every day, his eye is less likely to wander
too far for too long.

Sex isn't all there is to keeping the relationship, of course.
There's always romance. What! you say. Why, you've gone
through nearly this whole book without once mentioning romance! Not true: This book's philosophy is that there is no point

in looking for someone to "be romantic with." If all you really want are the mushy parts of the relationship, you aren't ready for one yet. HOWEVER: Once you have found somebody with whom you have terrific sex, and who you don't wish would turn into a pizza after sex, and with whom you find yourself having shockingly intimate and exciting conversations, well . . . now it's time for romance. Romance, for the purposes of this book, consists of the extra little things two people do for each other *after* they've constructed a relationship. And if there's one thing that seems to happen all too often after people move in together, it's that the romance dries up.

If you're both keeping yourselves up, physically and otherwise, and both working hard to keep the other partner interested, chances are you won't need any lessons in romance. It will be perfectly obvious to you that you should bring home flowers on Friday, subtly figure out his weekend plans ahead of time so as to be able to surprise him with a weekend getaway that will delight and will not inconvenience him, mail him a nice card even though you live together, and all the other little things that make up *true* romance.

Be original! Don't bring him a dozen red roses, or a box of candy. The real definition of "romantic" is "attentive," i.e., you are *paying attention*. If he idly says one day that he loves irises, don't rush out the next day; wait a few weeks and then surprise him with a bunch of those very flowers. You get double brownie points for both paying attention and remembering weeks later. (If you have to write it in your Daytimer to remember it, do it! He doesn't need to know.)

Find out a little more about what he does for a living without having to ask him; most people don't have all the tools they need to do their job. Find something he can use at work and give it to him. It's more romantic than it sounds!

If he has E-mail at work, send him a poem—you don't have to write it, just take the time to pick one that's good and type it up on your computer. It's not just the thought that counts—it's the effort you put into it.

All these things have a single cumulative effect: They constantly remind him that you are not taking him for granted. Think about it: How do extramarital affairs get started? People fall into routines; they go to work, come home, chat about work, eat dinner, maybe have sex (probably not), fall asleep in front of the TV. You don't think you're losing interest in your mate, but if you're not expressing interest, what is he to think? Especially when he meets that hot young pup at the gym, or in the mail room, or on the subway, who stares at him like . . . well, like you used to, many moons ago. A hot young pup *who is interested in him*! Who wants to know all about him, to touch him, to excite him, to . . . well, to make your partner need him the way you made your partner need you once upon a time.

Vary your routine. If you play tennis together every Saturday, great. One Saturday morning, get in the car and take him on a beautiful scenic drive to a tennis court fifty miles away. If you can afford it, do your weekend shopping one weekend at the expensive gourmet supermarket instead of Safeway, or take him to the nearest farmers' market. Your relationship together should be an adventure. Adventure, after all, is what romance is really all about.

6

The In-Laws Principle

No marriage worth its salt is free of conflict. Sooner or later you're going to argue about where to take your vacation, or whose family to spend the holidays with, or what to do with that big bonus one of you just got, or maybe even something worse. And you're going to need someone to talk to. Now, being a gay man, this means not just asking Mother for advice, but also your great big extended gay family. After all, there are a lot of things in gay relationships that Mother just can't help out with (and some that might make you queasy to talk to Mom about, frankly). Your extended gay family can be a treasure chest of advice for you; you can turn to them because they've experienced what you're going through.

However, gay or not, people tend to manifest into certain types when you ask them for advice. It's the **In-Laws Principle:** People often give you the advice they hope will get you to do what they want you to do. Herewith, the four types of advisers:

The Stand-by-Your-Man Type: This guy is probably married himself, and is the type to work hard at his relationship—maybe too hard. He's the type to stay with hubby whether hubby is doing right by him or not, because he's "committed to the relationship." He may also have a chip on his shoulder about being a gay man in a relationship; maybe he needs to prove something to the world about how two men can stay together. He's always going to advise you to stick it out, through any situation short of physical abuse. You need to take his advice with a grain of salt.

The Other-Fish-in-the-Sea Type is the polar opposite of the Stand-by-Your-Man type. This guy is probably single, and his advice is going to be to ditch the sucker at the first sign of trouble. That's what he's always done, after all—which is probably why he's still single. Frankly, this guy doesn't know much about relationships because he's never gotten very far into one. Take the other grain of salt with his advice.

The Sob-Sister Type: This guy thrives on crises. He'll be there for you, all right—constantly. There's nothing he likes more than to have someone run to him and sob on his shoulder. He'll tell you your mate is a beast if he thinks that's what you want to hear. He's not much for advice, but he's helpful: With him, you can do all the screaming and crying you don't want to do in front of your mate. Once you're done with him, you can move on to . . .

The True Friend: This is the guy who knows you pretty well, and who ought to know your spouse reasonably well, too (if you obeyed the **Cosmo Girl Principle,** that is). He's probably been with you through more than one relationship, so he's got a little perspective. He knows you well enough to grasp what you're getting out of this relationship, and even if there's something very wrong, he realizes there's nothing he can say that's going to get you out of it unless you truly want out. If anyone is really going to help you, it's this guy. If you've got a friend like this, it's in moments like this that you wonder why you never married him (no sexual attraction, probably).

7

The Joan Rivers Principle

Most of your little conflicts can be solved by applying the **Joan Rivers Principle.** At a certain part of her routine, Joan would be just about to say something really wild, maybe even shocking, and she'd ask her audience, "Can we talk?"

Communication is the heart of relationships. When you start out, everything seems obvious—you look into each other's eyes and know all you need to know. He touches you, and it always feels like the right touch at the right time. What is there to talk about?

But if you've ever had a relationship before, you know it doesn't stay that way. The longer you're with someone, the more you realize that you aren't the identical twins you thought you were when you first met. One day, to your enormous surprise, he does something that irritates the hell out of you. And worse, a couple weeks or even days later, he does it again! You (wisely) held your tongue the first time, but now that a pattern is developing, it's time to say something. The primary interpretation of the **Joan Rivers Principal** is: *Don't seethe.* Don't stew in your own juices. Don't grit your teeth and bear it. Sooner or later this will drive you crazy!

If you're having a hard time getting him to sit down and talk seriously with you about these things, make an appointment. Seriously—tell him that at seven P.M. on Thursday, the two of you are going to sit down and talk about what's bothering you. Don't be the least bit surprised if your revelation about what he's doing that's getting to you prompts him to reveal what you're doing that's bothering him! Irritation, like communication, is a two-way street. Don't get defensive; don't say what he doesn't like about your behavior doesn't compare to what you don't like about his. Don't argue with him! If something irritates him, you're not going to talk him out of being irritated.

Getting some counseling sounds like a drastic step. You might think to yourself, "That's what people do who are about to split up." But an ounce of prevention is worth a pound of cure. If the two of you find you can't discuss your issues without it devolving into an argument, a neutral third party could be the best thing. At least pick up a book like *Permanent Partners* by Betty Berzon, an invaluable volume that could just tell you what you're *really* upset about in the relationship.

▼8
The Joint-Checking Principle

It's tough to keep a relationship together without that piece of paper. It's been noted and quoted again and again that a straight couple married one hour have more rights than a gay couple together twenty-five years. Sometimes the need to prove your love and cement your relationship becomes overwhelming, and sometimes that small ceremony attended by a few close friends isn't enough. That's when you start thinking about having what *they* have—and really, what they have that we don't is a legal entanglement.

Moving in with someone is a big deal, but it's reversible if things don't work out. However, once you get into things like joint checking accounts and co-ownership of property, you're committing to the relationship in a manner far deeper, in some ways, than any exchange of rings. If things go wrong, it's no longer as easy to call it off, which is exactly why some couples do it, as a sort of "insurance policy" that they won't break up at their first fight.

Listen: Making it hard to break up is not the way to stay together. Think about it—if you really feel the need to do these things in the first year of your relationship, maybe you're doing them for the wrong reasons. If you're that nervous about your future with this guy that you feel the need to chain yourself to him financially, isn't that a sign that you see trouble ahead?

Eventually you want to have what straight folks have—community property, but you should want it as a sign that things have gone so well with the two of you that your future together seems as assured as it can be.

Start slowly: During that first year that you live together, there are plenty of reversible things you can do that are slow steps toward total financial conjoinment, if that's what you really want. Name each other as the beneficiary on your life insurance policies; change your will; make out a medical power of attorney. If your relationship smashes up, all these things can be reversed in a day.

On your first anniversary, step back and evaluate the relationship: Is this someone you want to spend the rest of your life with? If you are still divinely happy after living with this guy for a year, well, chances are good that he's the one. You'll know him well enough by then to know if he's going to empty the joint checking account for an impulse purchase, or declare bankruptcy after the two of you have cosigned for a loan for that big BMW.

It's hard enough to split up when joint property is involved, harder still when there are other living creatures to fight over. Again, don't think that buying a pet together is going to cement your relationship. And God forbid you adopt a child before you've been living together in relative harmony for several years. Remember that while it's just the two of you splitting up, the trauma extends only as far as the two of you; add pets and/or kids and you're involving others in your crisis.

▼IV

THE STAR-CROSSED LOVERS' GUIDE TO LIFE

Okay, okay, I admit it: I glossed over one of the biggies in the first edition of this book. Sure, it covered compatibility, sexual and otherwise, but the closest I got to addressing some of the real obstacles to a long-term relationship was the **In-Laws Principle,** which suggested that there might be people in your life who'd like to derail your relationship, for whatever reason.

But there's more than one way to sink two ships passing in the night, to mix a metaphor or two. Sometimes true love comes attached with some pretty significant obstacles—such as age, money, and of course "your (or his) past." In many ways, these are more of a problem to the people outside your relationship, but unless the two of you are planning to live on a desert island cut off from the outside world, you're going to have to face the fact that what other people think of your relationship is going to color what you think of it. And isn't it hard enough just having a *gay* relationship, let alone having to deal with other objections?

The following new sections are intended to help you get past all that. Remember that if it *is* love, it doesn't come around very often, and sometimes you get everything you ever wanted, only it doesn't always look the same way it looked in the catalog.

The *Rich Man, Poor Man* Principle

Andrew Holleran had it pegged when he wrote in *Dancer From The Dance* that on the dance floor, there was a "democracy [of] erotic love," where "the boy passed out on the sofa from an overdose of Tuinals was a Puerto Rican who washed dishes in the employees' cafeteria at CBS, but the doctor bending over him had treated presidents." Out in the bars, in the dance clubs, even more so in the sex clubs, where the towels all come from Costco and there are no designer labels to flaunt, gay men are all equal.

But you, having picked up this book, are looking for a man whom you will see more than occasionally with his clothes on. We've all gone home with someone who apologized in the cab, "The place is a mess," and we let it slide. After all, "the place" could be a by-the-week hotel in the bad part of town, or it might be a house that fell out of *Architectural Digest* along with the slip cards; "a mess" could mean roaches that flee like The Blob when the light comes on, or a single glass left unwashed in the industrial kitchen, glaring malevolently at its owner from a tastefully spotlit sink.

But that's just sex. Numbers are exchanged the next morning under any circumstances, but when your number beeps a pager and his is picked up by an answering service rather than an answering machine, chances are that "I'll call you" won't mean "I'll call you back."

The ***Rich Man, Poor Man* Principle** begins with a daring assumption: People with money tend to search for their mates almost exclusively among other people with money. Now, every single rich person in the world will say out loud, "I'm not rich!" Sometimes this is because they're afraid they'll be taken advantage of by poor people; sometimes it's because their perspective is so skewed and they are so afraid of being poor that they'll never have enough money to feel secure. To find out if you really are a rich person, just take this simple test:

1. A person with ten million dollars is
   a. a high net-worth individual.
   b. rich as *$%&^*.

2. A person whose family has had money all his life
   a. comes from a good background.
   b. was born with a silver spoon in his mouth.

3. A person who got rich
   a. made money the old-fashioned way—he earned it.
   b. made money the old-fashioned way—he stole it.

All done? How did you score? Well, if you answered "b" to all three questions, doll, you are *not* rich. If you answered "a" to all three, you're better off looking for your husband at black-tie-and-$100-a-ticket affairs rather than at Sunday beer busts.

However: Every now and then, despite all the obstacles (ruthlessly detailed below), a rich man and a poor man fall truly, madly, deeply in love, and make it work. It requires true love, a complete disregard for the opinions of others (and an exquisitely delineated prenup helps a lot), but it does happen. Two people find in each other the keys to their locks, and are unafraid to visit the locksmith to have duplicates made.

But capitalism universal and triumphant (with a little help from Charles and Diana) has banished the Cinderella fable to the dustbin of history, unless of course Cinderella can do some research on the Internet and find a few unclaimed savings accounts. Almost nobody will smile indulgently at your troth and sigh out loud that "love conquers all." Love, and $2.85, will get you a double mocha at Starbucks.

So, the two of you should be prepared for certain obstacles. Each of these is presented differently, as each of you will face them differently, depending on what side of the equation you're standing on at any given time. Of course, don't skip over the other guy's dilemma to get to your own—remember that a real relationship is about understanding, and it helps immeasurably if you know what he's going through, too.

The In-Laws: Face it—if you're poor, in their eyes, his money has just become their responsibility. They want to see him end up with someone who's got his own money, someone, in short, who'll make a hash throwing his own away in time for them to stop the interloper from emptying their dearly beloved's coffers, too. In their eyes, you are not a person but a potential black hole who might not even be able to tip properly, let alone refrain from dipping into capital.

If there's a *lot* of money involved, a palimony agreement will save you some of their ire and save both of you grief later, but there is more than just money involved: People with money often don't like to associate with people without it. It makes them uncomfortable. You, after all, are not quite a familiar creature, obsessed as you are with your base animal needs like paying the rent and still having enough left for groceries.

If you're the one with the money, congratulations: You haven't let your bank account or your family or your friends dissuade you from loving someone who is actually acquainted with the phrase "insufficient funds."

You know your family has your best interests at heart, especially when that interest is compounded. Any well-off person who's been young and has sown his oats has run into an opportunist interested in only one thing: money. As a gay man, you're a little more secure than your aunt Frieda, who has only her title of Countess Divot to show for the millions her husband spent on the ponies, polo, and otherwise. With marriage in America having been so well-defended by the divorced adulterers in Congress from your insidious onslaughts, your assets actually remain in your name after you set up with someone, unless you are fool enough to ignore the **Joint-Checking Principle** elsewhere in this book.

Some well-off people have decided that it's just better not to love someone without money than to run the risk of losing their own. They have not had the advantage of all-night conversations with your beloved, have never seen him with animals or children, and certainly haven't had the kind of sex with him that you've had. As a consequence, they don't like him as much as you do. Rather than trying to make them see what you see, accept that they will have to spend as much time with him over the years as you have in the much shorter time span since you met, before they can see him as you do. And they may never get over their prejudices, or they may just not like him. Who are you going to live with? Them or him? Your call.

"What Will My Friends Think?": I once dated a well-off, intelligent man, who'd been raised on a farm in Minnesota and still lived in the country there. He told me a story about his previous relationship with a man he'd met in San Francisco while on a visit. A long-distance relationship soon blossomed, but when the time came for him to meet the other guy's friends, they were prepared to roll him just on the strength of the "M" word on his driver's license.

Sooner or later, as it will in tony circles when debating where to eat dinner, the subject of sushi came up. When my naïve friend admitted he'd never had sushi, their combined raised eyebrows could have supported a suspension bridge. Being a gay man in his thirties, he was adjudged deficient in one of the major areas on "The Test," that floating questionnaire that determines whether or not you get your gay card (you know, such as "Have you ever done drag; have you ever seen *Beaches;* didn't you love *Beaches;* what do you *mean* you hated *Beaches!?*"). He was too flustered and shocked and embarrassed at the time, but as he later said to me, "I live in *Minnesota*. It's in the *Midwest*. It's not exactly a good place to get fresh ocean fish!"

No matter. If his friends are the kind of queens who go into cardiac arrest at the sight of the wrong shoes (or, on the other side of the equation, the big butches who snicker out loud at cashmere sweaters), you have to wonder what he's doing with you. Why would he pick someone to love romantically who is so unlike the people he's chosen to love as friends? We often choose our lovers on the strength of today's desires, but we choose our friends for life. If his are so different at their core from you and your friends, not in terms of tastes and culture, but in terms of heart and open-mindedness, you have to wonder if maybe the relationship is shallower than the deeper ones that will last.

Just remember the story of William Randolph Hearst and Marion Davies. Let's call it the ***Citizen Kane* Principle**: He had the money not only to defy society but to force society to pay call on his new wife, "the showgirl." But paying call is not the same as befriending, and Hearst's obsession with social standing meant Davies was no longer able to associate with her old crowd. Think of that scene in *Citizen Kane* where the two fictional counterparts argue in a vast empty room in front of a vast empty hearth. You need to be sure this man can take people as they are—not where they are from, or who are their people, or how much have they got. Otherwise, it'll be you screaming in front of that vast empty hearth.

▼2
The *Good Will Hunting* Principle

If there's one big mistake that people make when falling for someone from another social strata, it's keeping your prejudices about the rest of that group even as you toss them aside when you're with him, "the exception." Call it the *Good Will Hunting* **Principle:** You can't take the apple of your eye and expect never to see the rest of the bushel basket again. You can't keep your prejudices about "his type of people" after you come to know and love him, as if he were the "special exception."

You may find yourself feeling uncomfortable around his friends at first, especially if you start to dwell on surface differences between you and them, like money and taste. If they are good people, they will wait for you to show them who you are, instead of deciding who you are based on your "crowd."

The *Maurice* Principle

At the end of E. M. Forster's *Maurice,* our rich and privileged floppy-haired hero is to be found with his gamekeeper lover out in the woods, having taken "A Passage to D. H. Lawrence Land," the two of them living happily ever after chopping wood and looking more like the Smith Brothers every day.

A lovely ending to a fairy tale, but in reality, if one of you has money and the other does not, chances are you will end up residing closer to the higher standard of living than the lower. The one with more money will simply not see any reason why the two of you should share a place you can both afford, when you could just go ahead and share a place only he could afford. Inequality in any relationship is the first crack in the vase of roses. (Come on, you never saw *A Star Is Born?*) If one has more money, and pays more rent, he has more power in the relationship. He may *say* it doesn't matter, but the fact is, if he's not willing to go movin' on down, from the East Side, from his dee-luxe apartment in the sky-y-y-y, he's not willing to give up the advantage in the relationship that gives him.

▼4

The Patron of the Arts Principle

Now, every relationship is in some way transactional. You give, I give; you get, I get. Maybe the things that you give me that I value most are love, great sex, and someone to help me manage the little details of my life, and the things I give you that you value most are love, a pleasant home, and the stability and freedom to pursue long-term goals. As long as love is the number one on both lists, there's nothing wrong here.

In the eyes of the outside world, supporting someone while he goes to school is one of the most respectable ways of conducting a financially inequitable relationship. Of course, if the beloved is studying photography at the New School and churning out "interesting" photographs of manhole covers, some people might start seeing the whole school thing as a mere front for a "kept boy" relationship. But then again, art being what it is today, those manhole cover shots might end up making him more money next week than *Vogue* cover shots.

It's also worth remembering the "Mrs. M.D." experience: More than one woman has worked her fingers to the bone to get hubby through medical school only to be ditched once he was suddenly the one with the position and the paycheck. If it's a "loan," put it in writing, or be prepared to write it off (and not on your taxes, either—your partner still doesn't qualify as a dependent no matter how dependent he may be).

And finally, the Golden Rule: Prenups keep things on the up and up. It's that simple. Palimony happens, and if it can happen to Liberace and Rock Hudson, it can happen to you. If the whole money thing is clear from the start, there's less likely to be arguing over it later. When relationships fall apart, people start arguing over the tacit agreements, not the spoken ones. What was once an unspoken area of common understanding suddenly becomes a gray area open to (legal if not judicial) interpretation, not to mention a whole lot of George and Martha–style drinking and mudslinging. Put it in writing, or "Show Me the Money."

5

The *Harold and Maude* Principle

Gay relationships spend more time under the microscope than straight relationships; while a fifty-something CEO may well encounter a raised eyebrow or a behind-the-back chuckle when he bags his twenty-something trophy wife, in most eyes he's done something not only acceptable but admirable, a proof of his potency. Yet send a fifty-something gay man and his twenty-something companion to the same party as the straight couple above, and the one is a dirty old man who won't let go of his pursuit of youth and the other is a gold digger willing to have sex with that wrinkled old thing in exchange for what he can get out of him—and it's not just the straight couples whispering that, but other gay men, as well.

Like richer and poorer, there are public challenges to this kind of relationship and private ones, too. In fact, most people view an older/younger relationship as necessarily mercenary. And while far more older gay men are attracted to younger ones than vice versa, there a few young men who are into older men, not one in a million but few enough that they can choose their potential partners the way bears can dine leisurely on salmon swimming up river. And like Harold and Maude of the film, they have to be prepared for the shock and criticism they will get for not swimming with their own kind.

The public challenges to this relationship are the same as those to a richer/poorer one: basically, "What will people say?" Friends and family of both partners will question the other's motives; you will probably be awkward with each other's friends at first (though for different reasons than richer and poorer, as we'll see), and there is almost always an economic imbalance between someone established in the world and someone just making his way. Here it's the private ones that are the real challenge to making the relationship work and continue.

6

The *Primal Fear* Principle

What an older man has to look out for first and foremost is the *Primal Fear* **Principle**: As my shrink once told me after a disastrous relationship with a younger man, "There are indeed many young men out there who are more mature than their peers and want a relationship with someone older, but there are also a lot of young gay men out there who are angry with their fathers and are going to be transferring that rage to every man they have a relationship with." He may seem like the world's sweetest boy, and he may lavish you with admiration and respect at first, but beware: If he turns into quite another person the first time you neglect to put him first, it's time to start watching more closely for what may be seething beneath the surface. Most older men examine the motives of young men solely on a financial basis, and if there is no danger there, they relax. If there is no hidden financial motive, usually there is no hidden motive at all, but it's best to find out as much as you can about a young man's relationship with his father before you hand him the keys.

Most every relationship starts with a physical attraction, and while older and younger often meet and develop their attraction afterward, chances are they are still going to go hot and heavy at the start of their physical relationship. However, an older man can give himself a backache trying to keep up sexually with a younger one. In most relationships, as I have said elsewhere in this book, the sex dries up after a while; but in this kind of dynamic, the younger partner is going to be more likely to want sex with someone, after the older one has settled into a less exerting sex life. An open relationship on the sexual front is something to consider if you want to keep the rest of the relationship together.

▼7

The *Zelig* Principle

Then there's what I call the ***Zelig* Principle**. In my novel *Every Man for Himself,* John, the thirty-something protagonist, falls for Brian, a twenty-one-year-old. But as the relationship develops, John realizes there are certain rivers over which bridges can't be built, and the river of time is one of them. John narrates to his friends how he'd picked up a techno-music compilation CD and on examining the sleeve discovered it was from K-Tel. He laughed out loud and showed it to Brian, who didn't get the joke, not having been around in the 1970s when K-Tel sold compilation albums "only available on TV" (you know, albums—the black things, made of vinyl). These records featured all the latest AM-radio hits—only the songs were all covers, as performed by studio musicians under the cheesy "band" name "Sessions." It was like buying your very own bad lounge act, without the "Thank you, you're wonderful" at the end of each song.

The point being, an older person has cultural references that simply cannot be translated or explained to someone who didn't live through the experience. They can know the facts you're referencing, but not the state of mind at the time; how something that would be laughed off the market today was so popular back then, that only a handful of people knew *then* that it was cheesy, and that knowing it was cheesy was what we used to identify each other.

In Woody Allen's satire *Zelig,* his character somehow manages to be at the right place at the right time to experience everything important. People of a certain age still ask each other, "Where were you when you heard that Kennedy was shot?" It's a question that brings them together instantly, but it means nothing to those of us who weren't born or were too young to know what was going on. But it's a combination of these questions, serious and frivolous, Kennedy and K-Tel, that lets people of the same age build contacts with each other faster than people whose formative years were spent in very different psychological climates.

As I had a friend of John's put it in *Every Man for Himself:*

"The irony is," Matt thought out loud, "that kids these days may have more in common with the kids in the '60s than they do with us. Kids in the '60s had marijuana, free love, straight hair, Woodstock, and the Kennedys; today they've got marijuana, free love, straight hair, Woodstock II and . . . Clinton, but still!"

"And we got crack, AIDS, Joan Collins, arena rock, and Reagan," John added. "Why do I feel so cheated?"

The important thing for the older one in the relationship to remember is the old saw about "having to walk to school ten miles in the snow and twenty miles back." You can't criticize someone younger for not knowing how it felt when you were young, for not living through a Depression or a World War or the worst days of AIDS. And though I did it in my novel, try not to tell them how lucky they are and how good they have it compared to you. It only makes you sound like a cranky old queen.

This is where a May-December romance can benefit both parties enormously; the younger gets the benefit of the older one's life experience, and the older gets the benefit of the younger one's fresh eyes to see the world through the lens of *now* rather than *then.*

▼8

The *Out of the Past* Principle

If you're in love, you've stayed up all night talking with your beloved at least once, telling each other your histories and your hearts' desires. And while some of us have had to learn not to blurt out all our secrets on the first date, most people tend to reserve certain information about themselves until later on, when they feel safe enough with their beloved to spill it all.

Sometimes these secrets take the form of past deeds or misdeeds; other times they take the form of past loves who are not entirely in the past, whether by your choice or your ex's. There are some secrets that may end up being buried and left for dead—secrets that if revealed by you wouldn't help the relationship, but if revealed by others wouldn't really hurt it—just old embarrassing moments, mostly. But then there are other secrets that, if revealed, could change your beloved's entire attitude about you, or at least leave him feeling hurt that you never felt secure enough with him to tell him.

▼9

The *Striptease* Principle

More than one attractive, young gay man has been presented with the opportunity to spin his flaxen hair into gold. While many have spurned the opportunity for a variety of reasons (he didn't want an appearance in a porn flick kiboshing a real acting career later on; he didn't want his mother to see him naked in *Playgirl;* he'd seen his old high school math teacher at a gay strip club once and didn't want the old dear pottering into another one someday and seeing him on the stage), there's only two reasons he decides to do it, after all: It's fun and easy for him, or he really, really needs the money.

Is it really necessary to tell your beloved everything you've ever done? Especially if you've never been arrested for it! Well, you wouldn't want to go to a cocktail party and discover that his best friend was the guy who used to show up at Interludes every Wednesday night to stuff a tenner in your jockstrap—at least, not if you hadn't already told your sweetie about your no-collar career. And if you've ever been in a porn flick or skin mag, rest assured that somehow, someday somebody is going to recognize you and say, "That was my favorite magazine/movie ever! I still whack off to you all the time!" Your partner may be amused, turned on by the thought of you idolized by others, or flustered, embarrassed, and angry that you never told him.

When the time comes in your relationship to say the words,

"There's something I have to tell you," you'll be familiar enough with his attitudes to know how to approach the subject. You may just decide it wasn't a big deal and not bother to tell him, and if it ever comes up, just tell him you didn't think what you used to do to supplement your income was worth detailing. Remind him that he's probably done an embarrassing thing or two in the past himself, and that he would want you to be forgiving if his indiscretions ever came to your attention.

▼10

The *Clean and Sober* Principle

It's hard to find a gay man who hasn't experimented with drugs, and it's easy to find a gay man who's had a problem with them. Gay culture was formed by an outside world that condemned us to hell as hedonists, so naturally, gay men said, "Well, what the hell." Unfortunately, what a lot of us ended up doing was building a hell of our own as drugs became more important than anything or anyone.

In recovery, they teach you how to address your past when forming new relationships. You tell someone, "I had a drug problem." You don't tell them, "I used to shoot up speed and go out at night cruising parking meters and propositioning mailboxes." Recovery literature compares it to telling someone you're divorced—you don't have to give anybody the details of how or why it didn't work out, just that you're divorced.

What recovery doesn't teach you is how to separate sex from drugs, which is the biggest problem gay men with drug problems have. They can't have one without the other, at least they couldn't so far. You are urged not to try and form any relationships within the first year of your recovery, and rightly so. Addiction is a lean, mean rationalization machine, and there's no better way for two addicts to get back into drugs than for them to fall in lust. Especially two gay addicts who shared the same drug of choice, usually one of the "sex drugs" like crystal meth, Ecstasy, GHB, "Special K," etc.

So let's assume you're being practical enough to avoid getting together with someone who's recently had the same problem with drugs you've had. You've met a "normie," a person who either drugs recreationally (whom you will have to ask to stop doing them entirely if he's going to have a relationship with you) or who just doesn't do drugs at all. Telling him about your past won't be so bad if you've got a present he can measure against everything he things when he hears the words "drug problem." If you've got a place to live, an income, a circle of friends, an involvement in the community, chances are you're probably not doing drugs anymore (probably not; addicts are ingenious at hiding their behavior as long as possible, as you well know if you are one). You're probably involved in some kind of drug-recovery group where you've made friends who can readily testify to him that it's been a goodly while since you last darted bug-eyed in and out of their sight.

Again, it's up to you how much to tell him about the details. It's not exactly like a divorce; in the case of a divorce a potential new mate may very well want to know what went wrong in the last relationship in order to look for warning signs in this one. Moreover, when you go into the details of what you did as an addict when you're with other addicts, they tend to laugh knowingly, having done it themselves. The new boyfriend may not quite understand that the hours you spent combing through the carpet for drug crumbs are well behind you now, as long as you don't get high again.

Of course, it's complexities like this that lead many people in recovery to cruise meetings for mates (after that critical first year has passed, that is): Someone whose dark past mirrors yours needs no explanation. He is actually someone closer to you than a "normie" could ever be. As with those historical associations just mentioned in the last section, identical personal experiences bring people closer together more quickly.

Some people drop out of NA or AA meetings after they've been sober for a while; their desire is to be a "normie," someone who doesn't do drugs and never has to think about drugs. But if you and your new flame are both addicts, it behooves both of you to stay in, or return to, a program of meetings and support, because while you've learned to manage your own inner voice of addiction, now you're outnumbered 2 to 1. Your inner addict, and his, could gang up on each of you.

You can tell which recovery meetings are "cruisey;" they're the ones where half of the group goes outside for a cigarette at the break and doesn't come back, pairing off two by two into the night. This makes a lot of people in recovery indignant. Nonetheless, at least the people doing this are out looking for someone to go home with who isn't getting loaded—especially, since most of the places you scout for sex serve booze and/or offer dark places to get high.

The path to a long-lasting relationship for two recovering addicts is perhaps the most star-crossed of all, since resisting the urge to get loaded is an everyday battle for the rest of your life. Nonetheless, there are some battles that are easier fought with another by your side than without, and this is certainly one of them.

The *Guess Who's Coming to Dinner* Principle

Talk about a double doozy: the public trials of an older/younger couple, a richer/poorer couple, or just about any other couple are nada compared to what any interracial couple goes through on the streets—never mind a gay interracial couple.

Cultural conflicts add to the soup of obstacles the two of you must live with, be they Latin macho, African-American religious beliefs, or just good old-fashioned white Christian homophobia. People as a general rule want you to make it easy on them to accept you; if you present them with something doubly strange, they resent you for not trying hard enough to be familiar. Your friends and family may display the sort of internalized racism that would never be drawn out of them as an opinion of anybody else, but when they are now confronted with the alien brought among them to be accepted as one of them, even the best of them may hesitate a moment, confused by what to do. After all, just as you wondered what they would think of your beloved, they, in turn, are wondering what their friends and family will think of this stranger at their table.

If you're pure of heart enough to fall for someone regardless of race and the consequences that love will bring, sure, it's just plain irritating to see people around you who haven't been able or willing to take the same step. But getting angry at them and resenting their reservations or ignorance won't change anything. Sure, they're going to get so nervous about saying the wrong thing that they're going to be more likely to say it than if they just relaxed. But are you going to say, "*Aha!*" and rake them over the coals for it, or will you just smile indulgently, letting them know they messed up, and watch: them slow-roast over those coals instead? Putting people on the defensive reinforces their positions; even people who know they're in the wrong don't want to admit it under attack.

It's not for you to live the life of a saint, to be "an example" that makes such relationships acceptable. Lots of gay people, especially the coat-and-tie brand of gay-rights advocates, advocate our all living wholesome, dreary, minivan-driving lives just so that people will no longer be afraid of gay people as "different." Anybody who thinks you should live a life to avoid others' stereotypical images is just reviving that horrid old platitude about middle-class African-Americans being "a credit to their race."

Nevertheless, there is a brighter spotlight on you as an interracial couple. Even in people who aren't really prejudiced, a look will flit across their faces when they see you together, just because people get so accustomed to the familiar that the unfamiliar startles them.

12

The Long-Distance Principle

Well, I'd been doing pretty well with the movie titles, but I'll be damned if anybody has made a movie about a long-distance relationship. Then again, a love that takes place via E-mail and phone isn't exactly the kind of action that translates well to the screen.

There are two kinds of long-distance relationships, and only one of them works. The kind of relationship that starts out this way is going to sink; only the one that gets in some good face-to-face time at the start and then goes long distance can succeed. Take it from someone who's met too many men on the computer who were ideal, but from two thousand miles away. Someone you meet while he's on vacation, or a business trip, with whom you have a whirlwind affair, is not someone with whom you can develop a relationship. Or maybe the best way to put that is to say, he is not someone with whom you *should* develop a relationship. Everyone I've ever known who's gone into this kind of relationship has done so because the time they spent with the other person was so incredible that they immediately forsook all others and put all their eggs in one basket.

But focusing all your attention on someone who is, to put it simply, *not here,* is only going to make you lonelier *here,* and more dependent on that person, a person about whom you are not really learning a lot. A voice on the phone or a piece of E-mail gives you few clues about a person. It robs you of the opportunity to pick up on all those little signals people put out when they're with you, robs you of the chance to see them interact with other people and how they treat people whom, frankly, they don't want anything out of. The two of you build pictures of one another, and each time you get together again in person, these images ring falser each time. The only exception to this would be if one or both of you are amazingly well-off and can afford a plane ticket to reunite every weekend, but for the most part, these relationships take place without such funding.

However, if you do start to fall for someone, and one of you has to move or spend time away for some reason, choosing to carry on the relationship long-distance is a viable alternative. It's going to cost a lot of money in phone bills and plane tickets, but if you've found someone with whom you are really building something worthwhile, don't let it go just because one of you is being geo-graphically displaced.

The hardest part of this kind of relationship is keeping the ro-mance alive. This doesn't mean sending flowers or anything like that, but doing things that are more inventive, ways to feel close even if you aren't nearby. I once a had a long distance relationship (of the first, wrong kind, but it still gave me some good ideas) where I tried to think of things like "going to the movies together." We picked a movie and went to see it in our respective cities at al-most the same time, then called each other and talked about it as if we'd just seen it together. (I picked *Shakespeare in Love,* one of my all-time favorites, and a movie that surely was made for lovers. I should have known the relationship was doomed when he told me he didn't like it!)

Creativity is the key to keeping this kind of relationship going—all the little things you can do for someone in person (a look, a touch) aren't available. How are you going to make up for that? Send a lock of hair, make a videotape, send something of yourself across the distance to say, "We're still connected; I still love you; I will wait for you."

13

The Austin Powers Principle

Who? What the hell does Austin Powers have to do with star-crossed love? Well, if you've seen the movie, you'll remember that here's this ridiculously dressed guy, with bad teeth, talking about shagging all the time, and in the end he gets the girl. Austin's secret is that he never sees that people around him think he's a geek—he never even notices what they think because he's not looking. He knows he's a sexy shag, baby, and you should, too!

In all these star-crossed relationships, but perhaps most so in yours, the greatest obstacle the two of you face is learning not to care what other people think. Because the fact is, the facts don't matter. People believe what's most convenient for them to believe, and they tend to avoid or deny facts that would make for less convenient worldviews. You can't teach these people anything; you can't prove anything; you just have to let it go. People like that, when pressed, will finally say, "It's just wrong" because they don't have any real reasons at the core for their disapproving. They just need something to disapprove of, and the smallest minority they can find is always a handy target.

People also like to predict disaster; it's more fun than predicting a sunny day. And if you're in a relationship where the odds are against you (or seem so in their eyes), they're going to take the opportunity to generate a little excitement, to pull you aside to warn you not so much for your benefit but so they can go back to their other friends and say, "I pulled him aside and warned him, but he just wouldn't listen."

Stand by your man—and your guns. Love is a scarce commodity; hoard it. It never goes down in value.

In Conclusion

So now you've met Mr. Right, played it cool, given it time, let it grow, finally popped the question or had the question popped, married him, and lived happily ever after. Congratulations!

Okay, okay. Maybe you've just read this book, gotten a few ideas, and are ready to embark on the hunt again. Congratulations. Anyway, the important thing is that you *keep trying*. If you shut this book and take away only one thing, it should be: *Don't give up!* If you are really looking for a partner to share your life with (and not somebody to make it all better), you will find someone if you keep looking.

Stay positive! There's no bigger turnoff than someone who kvetches day and night about how "There are no good ones out there" or "They're all taken" or "All I date are jerks." If you're meeting only jerks, you're doing something wrong . . . or, worse, maybe you think jerks are all you deserve. The people who feel the worst about being single are usually those who don't have much of a life—busy people with lots of friends are enjoying life too much to get seriously depressed about the lack of a mate. As long as you *need* a man you're not ready for one.

The best way to meet Mr. Right is to be your own Mr. Right: If you want someone fit, successful, at peace with himself, active, fun-loving, and adventurous, then do what it takes to become such a person! After all, what kind of person do you think someone like that is looking for himself?

Actually, if you take only *two* things away from this book, the other should be: *HAVE FUN.* The whole point of this exercise is to find somebody to have fun with. If you assume a grim, desperate demeanor, treating this whole quest like some kind of awful burden, you're going to drive off all the good ones. This is an adventure! Everything you're doing to meet men is also an opportunity to make friends. (Okay, you're not going to make many friends at the sex club.)

Once you get him, remember it ain't over. He fell for you because you were sexy, fun, interesting, delightful. If you stop being all these things, why should you be surprised when he announces that he's leaving you for someone else who *is* all those things?

You've got to keep yourself up, and keep up your relationship, too. Don't think this means only going to the gym three times a week and eating Ben and Jerry's only on Sundays—your relationship needs exercise, too. Be spontaneous, creative, *adventurous*! Plan things you can do together, or that you can do for him (and if he's not reciprocating, remind him that this is his job, too).

Finally, don't go into anything thinking it's going to last forever. Sure, maybe your parents were together thirty, forty years . . . but they worked for the same company all their lives, too. How many jobs have *you* had already? Things change, people change—a good relationship will last many years, and many gay couples part amicably as their lives move in different directions. Enjoy it while it lasts, work to keep it going, but accept it when it ends . . . and get ready for your next adventure.

There aren't really any "Rules" for finding and maintaining relationships, only guidelines. One of the happiest couples I ever knew met in a sex club, so who knows? That other book isn't about building a relationship that's going to satisfy you—it's about trapping a man! This whole experience, this whole *adventure,* isn't about making someone your prisoner; it's about making someone your partner.

When you look back on what's been said here, you'll realize it's really just common sense. Use your head—it's your best friend.

Good luck—and enjoy the ride.

ABOUT THE AUTHOR

For three and a half years, Orland Outland was an entertainment columnist for San Francisco's gay papers *Bay Area Reporter* and *Frontiers*. He has also written for the *San Francisco Bay Guardian*, *San Francisco Review of Books*, and *Movieline*. He is also the author of *Death Wore a Smart Little Outfit*, *Death Wore a Fabulous New Fragrance*, and *Death Wore the Emperor's New Clothes*, a San Francisco-based mystery featuring a cross-dressing detective. His novel *Every Man for Himself* is now available in trade paperback from Kensington Publishing.